ReFocus: The Films of Kelly Reichardt

ReFocus: The American Directors Series

Series Editors: Robert Singer and Gary Rhodes

Editorial Board: Kelly Basilio, Donna Campbell, Claire Perkins, Christopher Sharrett, and Yannis Tzioumakis

ReFocus is a series of contemporary methodological and theoretical approaches to the interdisciplinary analyses and interpretations of neglected American directors, from the once-famous to the ignored, in direct relationship to American culture—its myths, values, and historical precepts. The series ignores no director who created a historical space—either in or out of the studio system—beginning from the origins of American cinema and up to the present. These directors produced film titles that appear in university film history and genre courses across international boundaries, and their work is often seen on television or available to download or purchase, but each suffers from a form of "canon envy"; directors such as these, among other important figures in the general history of American cinema, are underrepresented in the critical dialogue, yet each has created American narratives, works of film art, that warrant attention. *ReFocus* brings these American film directors to a new audience of scholars and general readers of both American and Film Studies.

Titles in the series include:

ReFocus: The Films of Preston Sturges
Jeff Jaeckle and Sarah Kozloff

ReFocus: The Films of Delmer Daves
Matthew Carter and Andrew Patrick Nelson

ReFocus: The Films of Amy Heckerling
Frances Smith and Timothy Shary

ReFocus: The Films of Budd Boetticher
Gary D. Rhodes and Robert Singer

ReFocus: The Films of Kelly Reichardt
E. Dawn Hall

ReFocus: The Films of William Castle
Murray Leeder

edinburghuniversitypress.com/series/refoc

ReFocus:
The Films of Kelly Reichardt

E. Dawn Hall

EDINBURGH
University Press

For Jason and Lucian, all of my love.

Edinburgh University Press is one of the leading university presses in the UK. We publish academic books and journals in our selected subject areas across the humanities and social sciences, combining cutting-edge scholarship with high editorial and production values to produce academic works of lasting importance. For more information visit our website: www.edinburghuniversitypress.com

Edinburgh University Press Ltd
The Tun—Holyrood Road
12 (2f) Jackson's Entry
Edinburgh EH8 8PJ

Typeset in 11/13 Monotype Ehrhardt by
Servis Filmsetting Ltd, Stockport, Cheshire

A CIP record for this book is available from the British Library

ISBN 978 1 4744 1112 7 (hardback)
ISBN 978 1 4744 1113 4 (webready PDF)
ISBN 978 1 4744 1114 1 (epub)
ISBN 978 1 4744 5224 3 (paperback)

Contents

Figures

Acknowledgments

I would like to extend my gratitude to *ReFocus* series editors Robert Singer and Gary D. Rhodes for their support, patience, and enthusiasm. At Edinburgh University Press, thanks are due to Rebecca Mackenzie, Richard Strachan, Gillian Leslie, Eddie Clark, and freelance copyeditor Camilla Rockwood. At Western Kentucky University, thanks are also due to Tim Brotherton, Merall Price, Dennis George, and David Lee for their support.

My undying gratitude goes to Linda Badley for her guidance and mentorship through the evolution of this manuscript. Many thanks also to Allison Adams, who assisted with the interview, Emily Gravette, Ryan Pait, and Emily Adkins for their many hours spent assisting on this project.

Thanks go to Claire Perkins and Con Verevis for including the *Old Joy* chapter in *Possible Films* (Edinburgh University Press, 2015) and to Katarzyna Paszkiewicz and Mary Harrod for including the *Meek's Cutoff* chapter in *Women Do Genre* (Routledge, 2017).

Many thanks go to Michael Lee and his students at the University of Oklahoma for inviting me into their incredibly designed Auteur course and for sharing their insights into Reichardt's work. I would like to thank Ted Hovet, my co-teacher and co-designer of the WKU Sundance Film Festival and Edinburgh International Film Festival courses, for his guidance and insight on my research and writing.

I extend many thanks to Neil Kopp for coordinating an interview with director Kelly Reichardt, and much appreciation to Ms. Reichardt for granting the interview and allowing its publication.

Finally, I would like to thank my family, Kitty Hall, Dee Powell, David and Janice Hall, and especially Jason Heflin and Lucian Hall-Heflin for their commitment, support, and love during the creation of this manuscript.

Academics have an opportunity, and I would argue an obligation, to influence the next generation of filmmakers, scholars, and critics by introducing them to a variety of diverse stories and storytellers. My hope is that I have contributed to diversifying the conversation.

CHAPTER I

Kelly Reichardt as Auteur

The challenge with this kind of filmmaking is turning all the limitations into something that works in your favor, something that adds to the frailty of the story itself.—Kelly Reichardt[1]

E ver since Laura Mulvey called for a feminist avant-garde cinema, feminist filmmakers and theorists have debated the merits of such a call and worked to either answer it or create a new understanding of feminist film.[2] While many contemporary women filmmakers shy away from the feminist label for fear of being pigeonholed at best and losing funding at worst, their work consistently highlights women's stories. Kelly Reichardt is no exception: she rejects the label of feminist filmmaker, but the feminist threads within her body of work, both in form and content, reflect a contemporary feminist filmmaking style, a rejection of mainstream filmmaking practices, a focus on gendered issues, and a subversive form that challenges cinematic pleasure.

Andrew Sarris, in his article "Notes on the Auteur Theory in 1962," drew on André Bazin's works to clarify auteur theory for American audiences, stating: "Over a group of films, a director must exhibit certain recurrent characteristics of style, which serve as his signature. The way a film looks and moves should have some relationship to the way a director thinks and feels."[3] While Sarris successfully incorporated and popularized the ideas behind auteur theory throughout film criticism, he also admits it is a difficult concept and plays into the hands of those who profit from classifications: "The task of validating the auteur theory is an enormous one, and the end will never be in sight. Meanwhile, the auteur habit of collecting random films in directorial bundles will serve posterity with at least a tentative classification."[4]As history shows, the labeling of filmmakers as auteurs has tended to be overwhelmingly weighted in favor of men. Feminist critiques of and resistance to concepts of auteurism stem from this historical exclusion of women filmmakers. Feminist scholars are divided between rejecting the label of auteur altogether, or working to rediscover historical women filmmakers and highlighting contemporary women filmmakers within the context of auteurism. Many argue that approaching women filmmakers as auteurs helps to make them visible. At the center of the auteur debate lies the question of what constitutes feminist cinema, but most agree that one of its qualities is a subversion of mainstream patriarchal cinematic norms.[5] Reichardt's auteurship stems from her distinct stylistic characteristics, including a subversion of commercial cinematic norms not only in terms of content, but also production methods.

Reichardt's films reflect a rejection of mainstream practices by sticking to micro-budgets, filming on location, and featuring deglamorized characters. Her means of production informs her content and her direction of acting; micro-budget filmmaking means that her shooting schedules are short, and necessitates creative troubleshooting that contributes to the aesthetic and content. In essence, a Reichardt film has consistent, recognizable features because of the very challenges that threaten to overwhelm the production and stand in the way of future films. Reichardt admits to believing every film will be her last, and over the years this tension has created an indie auteur. The film terms "independent" and "indie" tend to be used interchangeably by the mass media; however, they denote different categories. Michael Newman succinctly sums up the distinction by offering a historical view with contemporary adjustments, noting that American independent cinema since the studio system has used the term to discuss "production, distribution and exhibition outside the Hollywood studios," but the current "value of indie cinema is generally located in difference, resistance, opposition—the virtue of alternative representations, audiovisual and storytelling styles, and systems of cultural circulation."[6] In other words, while Hollywood initially defined independent film in terms of economic practices, the term has taken on a deeper cultural meaning, "making independence into a brand, a familiar idea that evokes in consumers a range of emotional and symbolic association."[7] While it seems that indie and independent are synonymous, indie survives as a branding mechanism denoting "fashionable cool" and acts as a "mystification of the more straightforward category 'independent'," thus "a distinguishing style or sensibility [and] a social identity."[8] In essence, a film can be categorized as indie without truly being created independently of studio or mainstream influence, and vice versa; the categorization lends itself to cultural context. As Newman articulates, "Determining what indie means requires that we be attentive to its cultural circulation as well as to economics, storytelling, and thematics."[9] Kelly Reichardt's films fall squarely into both independent and indie categories, notably due to content that reflects a contemporary social consciousness, but also because of her economic and production methods. The very act of filming outside and on location, with an emphasis on the environment in each feature, makes for political content, as seen in *Wendy and Lucy* (2008) and *Night Moves* (2013). While all of these production choices reject mainstream cinematic practices, Reichardt continues to attract Hollywood stars to her films. As she is known for creating minimalist, realistic "every person" characters, the prospect of a deglamorized role on a set offering little in the way of creature comforts does not seem to put actors off.

In a post-feminist era, many contemporary women filmmakers play down the issue of their gender in an effort to keep the focus of media attention on their work. In Reichardt's case, her work speaks volumes about her gender politics. As the analysis in this book will illustrate, most of her films have substantive roles for female protagonists, and even when women are not the main characters, gendered issues are addressed. *Old Joy* (2004), featuring two men, was touted at festivals as an LGBT film; it highlighted male friendship and feminized qualities such as sensitivity, vulnerability, and openness, which are often absent from Hollywood films. *Night Moves* features a male protagonist, but with strong female characters and a plot revolving around environmental concerns, the film reflects ecofeminist values. While the dangers surrounding poverty and economic downturn do not exclusively affect one sex, women are much more at risk than men when resources are scarce, as shown in *Wendy and Lucy*. Reichardt highlights social injustice, bias, and taboo topics in all of her films by means of her content, but it is the combination of her storylines and film form that contributes to her auteur qualities and establishes her avant-garde, feminist leanings.

Reichardt's work not only answers Mulvey's call to challenge mainstream cinematic pleasure; her films also introduce alternative forms of pleasure through slow cinema and an immersive experience with her characters. Slow cinema, as articulated by Matthew Flanagan in his work "Towards an Aesthetic of Slow in Contemporary Cinema," is not currently a term denoting genre, but as I will explore, the qualities of a slow cinematic film are collective and can be seen throughout Reichardt's body of work. Slow cinema is inherently political, since it resides in a nonconformist tradition:

> Although established forms of narration across national cinemas are always in a state of transition, a particularly striking dichotomy between mainstream continuity style and marginal art cinema has become increasingly apparent in recent years. The disparity has primarily emerged in the relationship between speed and editing, and now calls for a closer examination of the binary extremes of "fast" and "slow."[10]

Reichardt's work is in the art cinema tradition and its slow cinema characteristics contribute to this, as seen in her editing choices: "[E]xtended deferral of the imminence of editing opens a space for reflection on events, encouraging a contemplation of presence, gesture and material detail. In Theo Angelopoulos' words, 'the pauses, the dead time, give [the spectator] the chance not only to assess the film rationally, but also to create, or complete, the difference meanings of a sequence.'"[11] While *River of Grass* (1995) and *Certain Women* (2016) stand apart, with a faster tempo compared to her other features, all Reichardt's films pause for contemplation through long takes, lack of dialogue, and minimalist action—characteristics of slow cinema. In addition, both the aforementioned films display blatantly avant-garde qualities such as segmentation (the first via numbers and the latter via episodes). Reichardt consistently rejects the objectification of bodies through a mixture of realism and camera angles, and challenges audience expectations with lingering shots on seemingly inconsequential images after characters exit a scene. While the documentary-style quality of *Wendy and Lucy* and *Meek's Cutoff* (2010) is appealing, it is the tempo that tests viewers' attention spans, since most documentaries featuring social inequalities move faster. The quiet and authentic positioning of her complex characters aids Reichardt in offering alternatives to mainstream cinematic pleasure.

By all traditional definitions Kelly Reichardt is an auteur, but her work introduces a twenty-first-century contemporary woman-centered auteurship. Like many of her characters' stories, Reichardt's cinematic form and content serves to remind audiences there are alternatives to mainstream ideologies. Her films underscore the need to highlight unique and individualized human stories and she does this in realistic, often understated ways. Intentionally or unintentionally, Reichardt's filming style politicizes her cinematic form, allowing audiences time to digest her subtle, subversive messages. The dialectical dynamics within her body of work speak to the auteur characteristics Reichardt repeatedly incorporates into her form and content. Applying the auteur label positions her within a historical context among risk-oriented filmmakers who break from cinematic traditions and work outside the establishment. The resulting films expose spectators to innovative cinematic form and often to content that challenges the status quo. Reichardt's style of filmmaking creates space for engagement in contemporary issues, while her auteur qualities merge historical traditions with a twenty-first-century mindset.

NOTES

1. Kelly Reichardt, "*Old Joy* Director's Statement," Museum of the Moving Image Series *Adrift in America: The Films of Kelly Reichardt*, 3 April 2011.
2. Laura Mulvey, "Visual Pleasure and Narrative Cinema," *Screen* 16, no. 3 (1975): 6.
3. Andrew Sarris, "Notes on the Auteur Theory in 1962," in Barry Keith Grant (ed.), *Auteurs and Authorship: A Film Reader* (Hoboken: Wiley-Blackwell, 2008), p. 43.

4. Ibid. p. 44.
5. Karen Hollinger, *Feminist Film Studies* (New York: Routledge, 2012), p. 231.
6. Michael Newman, *Indie: An American Film Culture*, ed. John Benton (New York: Columbia University Press, 2011).
7. Ibid.
8. Ibid.
9. Ibid.
10. Matthew Flanagan, "Towards an Aesthetic of Slow in Contemporary Cinema," *16:9 Film Journal* 6, no. 29 (2008), <http://www.16-9.dk/2008-11/side11_inenglish.htm> (accessed 20 September 2017).
11. Mitchell quoted in Flanagan, "Towards an Aesthetic of Slow."

CHAPTER 2

A Closer Look: Kelly Reichardt

It's really hard to stay small, actually. That I've been able to make these last two films and have complete artistic freedom—what are you gonna trade that for?—Kelly Reichardt[1]

From childhood through her couch-surfing New York days to her most productive years thus far, Kelly Reichardt's life experiences have contributed to the methods she employs in her career as a director. Understanding her early experiences and preoccupations as they relate to her cinematic themes and characters helps to enrich a viewer's experience. Reichardt's brief reflections on her childhood, collected on the website *This Long Century*, reveal significant connections between her early years and her first feature film, *River of Grass* (1995).[2] In her debut Reichardt excels at introducing her native land, Dade County, and bringing its atmosphere to life. Todd Haynes, director and longtime friend, interviewed Reichardt for *Bomb*, and his introduction confirms the connection:

> *River of Grass* draws on stories and images from Kelly's own hard-boiled upbringing in suburban Florida. But unlike most movies drawn from personal experience, *River of Grass* roundly rejects the sentimentality and political correctness often associated with confessional dramas—particularly those which focus on women.[3]

Reichardt's debut features a female protagonist, Cozy. While Cozy's mother is only briefly mentioned in the film, her father figure's profession as a crime scene investigator seems to draw loosely on Reichardt's own childhood experiences: "My dad worked the midnight shift. His car had Dade County Crime Scene painted on the sides."[4]

During his interview with Reichardt, Haynes mentions that all the crime scene detectives in *River of Grass* feel as if they are "floundering in their careers," and that might be a result of Reichardt incorporating her own family dynamics to help shape her characters. Reichardt explains: "For my character [Jimmy] Ryder, it's the job that he fell into. My dad and his friends had that attitude. They were all crime-scene technicians, the guys who show up after the action. Their job is about solving a mystery rather than laying down the law—which is more up my mom's alley."[5] While she pokes fun at "crouching on the floor" of her mother's work vehicle, there is very little discussion about her mother's influence or involvement in Reichardt's life except in relation to her police work as an undercover narcotic agent: "My mom carried her holster in her purse and in a pinch was as likely to pull out a ratty hairbrush as a 38."[6] Since the justice system supported Reichardt's childhood home, it is not surprising that she used her father's real crime lab equipment as a set model: "The crime-scene office in the film looked like the one I used to visit when I was a kid. My dad brought all that stuff over to where we were shooting and helped Dave Doernberg, our art director, recreate the old office."[7]

Reichardt recalls splitting her time between her parents as a youth. She would stay with her father on the weekends, and that meant getting to know his four roommates, who were also divorced police officers: "They had these Sunday barbecues for all us kids who were with them on weekends. Their dates were always hanging around and everybody would be drinking and playing smilie-kill-ball in the pool."[8] Reichardt's semblance of family stability seemed to disappear after her parents' divorce, but her family grew when her father remarried; her second feature, one that failed to find funding, was based on her father and stepmother's initial meeting.[9] One indicator of family trouble is Reichardt's casual mention that her missing stepbrother was found during a trip to the local jail during the *River of Grass* shoot: "On day two they arrested our gaffer and confiscated all of our equipment. But that worked out for the best because when my dad went down to bail out Collin [the gaffer] he found my stepbrother who had been missing for a couple of weeks."[10] This seemingly off-topic and blasé admission happens while Reichardt is answering a question about police interference in her project and the difficulties she experienced trying to get through the short shooting schedule. Reichardt's work is shaped not only by the frustrations of filmmaking, but by the challenging family issues she has drawn on as inspiration.

Political ideas come into play in almost every interview with Kelly Reichardt about her life or work; similarly, her films reflect a concern about the state of America, touching on issues from the effect of specific presidential administrations, to corporate takeovers, to disaster preparedness. In an interview in 2006, Reichardt discussed the political implications of her second feature film: "*Old Joy* can stand for everything . . . The death of liberalism in America . . .

Old Joy has a feeling of my generation at a total loss."[11] Spectators might not immediately pick up on surface political motivations or messages when watching Reichardt's films, but with deeper reflection it becomes clear that they do incorporate strong political sentiments and questions. In another interview, she sheds light on what prompted her interest in politics: "[I]f you grew up in the Seventies you have a certain perspective. You have a sense of a certain justice or an ideal of liberalism during the Carter years as a positive phenomenon."[12] Reichardt's awareness of politics came early, so it is no surprise that it serves as a backdrop for most of her features.

As well as political commentary, representations of loneliness and instability are also pervasive in Reichardt's work. In *River of Grass* Cozy introduces her partner in crime, Lee, by commenting on loneliness: "I wondered if there was any other person on this planet that was as lonely as me; as it turned out there was, and he was living just a county away." Everyone in the film seems to be isolated and searching—as is Wendy, the protagonist in Reichardt's third feature, *Wendy and Lucy* (2008). Wendy lacks human support, a theme in the film, and by the end she gives up her dog Lucy to a better and more stable life, with the last shot showing Wendy leaving on a train bound for Alaska. However, Reichardt's work also illustrates that being lonely does not require being physically alone. In her fourth feature, *Meek's Cutoff* (2010), the protagonist, Emily, seems solitary even though she is always in a group. All three of these characters, whether alone or part of a group, convey a sense of solitude, a quality that might stem directly from Reichardt's experiences growing up:

> I remember Thurston Moore recalling when he was visiting Miami in those years, seeing an ad in the *Herald* that said, 'if anyone has heard of The Clash, please call me.' That really gets across the isolation and general feeling of being a teenager in an endless string of sunny days in a city of retired people.[13]

While regret is not an emotion her cinematic characters display, Reichardt seems to regret her own lost adolescent opportunities and experiences: "If only I could have stumbled into Andy Sweet's photographs or for that matter Stephen Shore's. Even if I had just seen some little bit of good art as a kid I think I could have had a whole different experience."[14] The inability to find relationships or role models to guide and encourage her art, such as photographers or musical artists, motivated Reichardt to search them out and eventually discover them; but the angst of her teenage years, the searching, loneliness, journey, and self-discovery, can be seen in all of her art.

If Reichardt has drawn on her own youthful experiences to make films, as evident in *River of Grass*, she also seems to be on a mission to depict marginalized people's experiences and frustrations—some of which are not unlike her own. In a 2008 interview with Reichardt, her fellow director Gus Van Sant comments on a theme of decay throughout her films: "[I]n *Old Joy*, the decay of their friendship [is a theme]. And the decay is strongest in *Wendy and Lucy*. Falling into this abyss of hopelessness."[15] Reichardt never agrees with his assessment, but does comment that the hopelessness she feels is conveyed in her endings. While there are elements of hopelessness, loneliness, and decay in her characters' relationships, Van Sant hints that they stem from Reichardt's personal experiences. Rather than Mother's Records or Blue Note Records, which are featured in *River of Grass*, Reichardt talks about her own early jobs in record shops, the lack of housing, and the decay of family structure:

Somewhere in the early 8os, having secured a job at Peaches Records and Tapes, I quit The Clog Shop on 163rd Street and dropped out of high school. I was no longer living at either of my parents' houses (they divorced when I was eight) but was bouncing around between my friend's parents' houses, my grandmother's condo in a retirement village and pretty much blowing it in every situation I landed. The order of things gets a little foggy here but I did get my GED and enrolled in Miami Dade Community College.[16]

She started taking pictures of Miami, and found encouragement for her art by winning sixteen dollars in a community college photography contest, but that did not stop her from moving north and destroying the photos:

Within a week of being in Boston I enrolled in night classes at Mass Art and when I was invited to flop on a couple of the art-school kids' couch, I was so totally fearful of them seeing my corny Miami photos that I destroyed them all. I remember tearing them up and throwing them in a dumpster . . . I felt a real need to disassociate myself with all things Miami.[17]

Many of Reichardt's interviews suggest that she felt as if she was growing up in a cultural wasteland, and her salvation was finding a supportive art culture in Boston and New York. No matter where Reichardt landed she found friends and support networks to help her, such as her collaborator Susan Stover: "When I first knew Kelly, she was a couch surfer . . . There were times when I kind of got worried, like, 'What's the end game here? What's going to happen?' It wasn't for six months she couch surfed, it was years."[18] Undoubtedly, this nomadic lifestyle helped inform the creation of Reichardt's characters, many of whom are also in liminal spaces searching for meaning and direction. *Wendy and Lucy* highlights a darker side of Reichardt's transient situation, in that Wendy does not have Reichardt's friendly support system. In an interview in *Slant* magazine, Reichardt is asked if Wendy's experience was based on hers: "I've been really broke . . . never hungry. I did live in New York for five years without an apartment, but I always ate. I've been as broke as Wendy, but I've always had more of a network of friends who were really generous to me."[19] That network of friends included talented artists, musicians, and filmmakers such as Jesse Hartman, Todd Haynes, and many others who ultimately supported each other through successful artistic collaborations.

While these connections served her well, in the *Slant* interview Reichardt also discusses how she grew her "technical chops," considering that she had very little formal film training: "[F]iguring out how to make films all came between the ten years between my two features . . . I never went to film school, I never studied any of that stuff. I'm a high-school dropout."[20] In reality, Reichardt is being modest about her skill and training. Speaking to Todd Haynes, she says she attended Tufts University's School of the Museum of Fine Arts in Boston, where she created a trilogy of Super 8 road movies. The themes apparent in her work, particularly that of the journey or quest, might stem from her early Miami years of searching for role models and artistic guidance, but they also developed from family interactions. In an interview with Sam Adams and the A.V. Club, Reichardt sheds light on why her films often revolve around journeys or searches, or have a "road movie" feel:

> It's a theme that started at the beginning [of my career], and I look back, and I guess it's just a good setup for different kinds of searching: question-asking, looking for the next place to go, what are you looking for, what are you leaving. All those things are good for grounding it in getting from point A to point B.[21]

The "searching" theme extends much further than physical movement, as all Reichardt's characters struggle to find themselves through inner journeys; and for many spectators, these inner searches resonate deeply. Her practical side is evident when she emphasizes the need to ground films "in getting from point A to point B"—and while she is referring to narrative devices, she is also referencing the human experience and struggle. Reichardt's family summer vacations tended to involve road trips, as she tells Adams:

> Ever since I was a kid, we had one of those piggyback campers where you could ride up in the bed . . . We would go from Miami to Montana pretty much every summer and take a different route out west . . . We would camp our way across the country. And as it's turned out, I continued doing that . . . [i]n my 20s.[22]

Reichardt takes as a starting point the universal desire to experience freedom, progression, and learning—all elements found in a road trip or journey—and allows her spectators to experience them through her films.

After graduating with a BFA from the School of the Museum of Fine Arts at Tufts and working as a prop assistant on Todd Haynes's film *Poison* (where the two first met), Reichardt was persuaded to start writing *River of Grass*. While they were co-directing a music video for the heavy metal band Helmet, Jesse Hartman suggested she write a script set near Miami. It was also a road movie with noir-detective threads, dark humor, and a feminist sensibility. Reichardt recalls her resistance to writing the script: "All through making the video Jesse kept talking about writing a script down in Miami . . . To me it was like, anywhere but there! It took me nineteen years to get out of Miami: I didn't want to go back."[23] After *River of Grass* and her first attempt at a second feature, both set close to her home, Reichardt would set her subsequent films in the northwest.

Like many of her characters, Reichardt has to struggle to assert herself and push past obstacles. Many of her early experiences while making *River of Grass* tested her, and may have contributed to her particular method of filmmaking. In an interview with *Bomb*, she discusses making her first feature film:

> I had written this script, lived with it and raised the money, yet I still had to go to the set each day and defend my post as director. It was the first time in my life that I was like, Oh, I get it, this is happening because I'm a five-foot-tall female—I wasn't given the benefit of the doubt . . . I fought for every shot in my film, which is such a drain and something I wasn't prepared for.[24]

While *River of Grass* was appreciated by reviewers (including one in *The Village Voice* touting it as "one of the year's smartest indies"), the positive reviews did not help Reichardt find funding for her next project, *The Royal Court*. She moved to Los Angeles in hopes of finding support for the film, but instead found multiple roadblocks and ultimately a dead end. She explained that in addition to being pegged as a "woman director" who created "women's films," the final nail in the coffin was that she had an African American female protagonist, and that acted "like double dynamite."[25] This type of attitude toward women directors and female protagonists is not new. Reichardt felt it sharply during her search for funding for *The Royal Court*: "[E]verything always started with, 'I don't make the rules.'"[26] Susan Stover, her associate producer on *River of Grass* and *Ode*, explained that Reichardt "was annoyed with herself that she went down that path, where 'I'll call you in a couple of days' becomes weeks becomes months becomes it never happens."[27] These difficult experiences motivated Reichardt to create independently of the studio system or even their "independent" branches. Abandoning feature filmmaking, she went back to Super 8 shorts with minimal crews, which helped to develop her minimalist aesthetic.

After *The Royal Court* was dropped Reichardt filmed *Ode*, her forty-eight-minute short based on Bobbie Gentry's song "Ode to Billie Joe," with a crew of four in one week: "There I was . . . standing outside in North Carolina with my good friend [Stover] holding the camera and hearing that loud lawn-mower sound, with two actors, just making something. It was just this huge epiphany: I'll just find another way to make films."[28] Following that philosophy, Reichardt went on to make *Then, a Year* (2002) and *Travis* (2004), two short films with little to no crew; but the desire to stay completely minimalist subsided when she was introduced to Jon Raymond's novel *The Half-Life*. In an interview with Gus Van Sant Reichardt comments, "It's my dream to someday make [*The Half-Life*] into a film but it can't exactly be done in any small way," and that "small way" is a hallmark of her filmmaking model. Keeping her costs low by adapting minimalist stories contributes to Reichardt's aesthetic and also reflects her earlier filmmaking trials: "The smaller-gauge work was freeing because there wasn't any expectation put on me."[29]

Another element of Reichardt's filmmaking model was her decision, at Todd Haynes's encouragement, to begin a teaching career. Teaching first at the School of Visual Arts in New York and then at Columbia and SUNY Buffalo not only brought Reichardt personal financial independence but helped her to continue her independent filmmaking, and culminated in a position as Artist in Residence in Film and Electronic Arts at Bard College. She told *Slant* magazine:

> Teaching has taught me a lot, it's put me around people who are smarter than me. It's turned me on to things to read that I wouldn't know to read. The students come in and they've traveled all over the world and they've read everything and they turn me on to stuff I just never caught on to.[30]

In short, Reichardt finds making low-budget films in a private way gives her the most satisfaction because it is lower risk and allows for artistic freedom and control. Teaching is one way she is able to sustain her creativity without soliciting Hollywood financing: "I was standing in a field with friends making [*Ode*]. It was like, how do I structure my world around this? *This* is satisfying. *This* is the pinnacle."[31] She added: "That's why I started teaching, I just said to myself, how can I sustain something . . . where I have some money to make some films."[32] Reichardt might be hinting at the co-opting of creative talent and vision into the more commercialized and marketable or "safe" content that Hollywood or its vintage branch studios require. While accepting studio funding might be easier, there is a high price to pay creatively for female filmmakers whose narrative films tend to feature thought-provoking content over action-packed storylines. And because Reichardt chooses to work with small independent production and distribution companies for all of her films (Glass Eye Pix, Filmscience, Oscilloscope, and others), she is able to continue making work while adjusting to fluctuations in the market or reduced opportunities.

Success for Reichardt means something very different than it does for more commercial independent filmmakers, or for those who work in the studio system. Through perseverance and hard work, she has shown that her micro-budget style of filmmaking can be extremely fulfilling: "I want to not have to go through development, to not have to deal with agents, to not have to deal with lawyers, to not have to show anybody my script, to not have to read script notes when I really don't want them, to not have anyone look at a cut of my film and then give notes when I really don't want them."[33] In other words, Reichardt's definition of success equals complete artistic autonomy, and so far she has thrived in this model. She prefers a private approach to filmmaking, as she reiterates in her interviews: "If you could make films and then put them out and not have to reveal anything about yourself, that would be, for me, total dream success . . . I don't like getting dressed up. I don't like getting my picture taken. I don't want to talk about myself. I like my privacy."[34] Success to Reichardt means creating art with no outside interference, and retaining a luxury that many filmmakers lose when funded by Hollywood: total control over their work. She may be one of the few who, as Jennie Rose has put it, have stopped using a patriarchal measuring stick for success, one of the "women creating stories, budgets and pictures, who go for a different brass ring or no brass ring at all. They've had to invent their own way to measure their worth."[35]

NOTES

1. Reichardt quoted in Ryan Stewart, "Redefining Success: An Interview with Kelly Reichardt," *Slant Magazine*, 5 December 2008, <https://www.slantmagazine.com/features/article/redefining-success-an-interview-with-kelly-reichardt> (accessed 20 September 2017).
2. "Kelly Reichardt," *This Long Century*, no. 190 (2012), <http://www.thislongcentury.com/?p=5570> (accessed 20 September 2017).
3. Reichardt quoted in Todd Haynes, "Kelly Reichardt," *Bomb* 53 (1995), <http://bombmagazine.org/article/1891/kelly-reichardt> (accessed 20 September 2017).
4. Ibid.
5. "Kelly Reichardt," *This Long Century*.
6. Ibid.
7. Reichardt quoted in Haynes, "Kelly Reichardt."
8. Ibid.

9. Haynes, "Kelly Reichardt."

10. Reichardt quoted in Haynes, "Kelly Reichardt."

11. Reichardt quoted in Michael Joshua Rowin, "Q & A: Kelly Reichardt, Director of *Old Joy*," *Stop Smiling Magazine*, 22 September 2006, <http://www.stopsmilingonline.com/story_detail.php?id=655> (accessed 20 September 2017).

12. Reichardt quoted in Vicente Rodriguez-Ortega, "New Voice: An Interview with Kelly Reichardt," *Reverse Shot*, 18 September 2006, <http://reverseshot.org/interviews/entry/804/kelly-reichardt> (accessed 20 September 2017).

13. "Kelly Reichardt," *This Long Century*.

14. Ibid.

15. Gus Van Sant, "Artists in Conversation: Kelly Reichardt," *Bomb* 105 (2008): 77.

16. "Kelly Reichardt," *This Long Century*.

17. Ibid.

18. Susan Stover quoted in Anne Hornaday, "Director Kelly Reichardt on *Meek's Cutoff* and making movies her way," *Washington Post*, 12 May 2011.

19. Reichardt quoted in Stewart, "Redefining Success."

20. Ibid.

21. Reichardt quoted in Sam Adams, "Kelly Reichardt and Jon Raymond," The A.V. Club, 26 April 2011, <https://film.avclub.com/kelly-reichardt-and-jon-raymond-1798225326> (accessed 20 September 2017).

22. Reichardt quoted in Adams, "Kelly Reichardt and Jon Raymond."

23. Reichardt quoted in Haynes, "Kelly Reichardt."

24. Ibid.

25. Reichardt quoted in Hornaday, "Director Kelly Reichardt on *Meek's Cutoff*."

26. Ibid.

27. Stover quoted in Hornaday, "Director Kelly Reichardt on *Meek's Cutoff*."

28. Reichardt quoted in Hornaday, "Director Kelly Reichardt on *Meek's Cutoff*."

29. Reichardt quoted in Van Sant, "Artists in Conversation."

30. Reichardt quoted in Stewart, "Redefining Success."

31. Ibid.

32. Ibid.

33. Ibid.

34. Ibid.

35. Jennie Rose, "Women in Film," *GreenCine*, 3 December 2011.

CHAPTER 3

Precursor: *River of Grass*

If we aren't killers, we aren't anything.—Cozy, *River of Grass*

These are not commercial films. But this way, the movie is done when I say it is . . . I have the kind of freedom you can only have by not taking too much money.—Kelly Reichardt[1]

Kelly Reichardt's first feature film, *River of Grass* (1995), is an interesting mix of realism and minimalism, but also demonstrates an experimentalism that aligns her with an older feminist counter-cinematic tradition. In her debut, Reichardt addresses theoretical film concepts such as the "male gaze" by emphasizing the female look, and employs Godardian techniques to remind viewers that they are watching a construction of reality. In interviews about *River of Grass* she details the work that went into a micro-budget film and explains the environmental and political messages woven through it. As with her later work, Reichardt's decision to stay completely independent affected the look, content, and popularity of the film; even more importantly, the production methodology of this first feature helped to establish her particular filmmaking methods and her auteur qualities.

PRODUCTION

Making a film is never simple, especially if it is a first feature, but micro-budget filmmaking has its own specific benefits and challenges. Reichardt has been able to retain complete artistic control over her films by working in the independent sector and making films with small budgets. She went into filmmaking with some experience, having worked in the art department on independent films such as Hal Hartley's *The Unbelievable Truth* (1991) and Todd Haynes's *Poison* (1991) as well as co-directing a music video for the heavy metal band Helmet. Reichardt recalls in an interview: "I worked on a lot of people's first film . . . I thought I could work this hard on my own film."[2] Reichardt's hard work paid off when *River of Grass* became one of the sixteen out of 600 entries accepted into the 1994 Sundance Film Festival.[3] The film was nominated for the Grand Jury Prize in the dramatic category at Sundance, and two years later Reichardt and her lead actress, Lisa Bowman, were nominated for several more—at least five nominations in total, although none was awarded.[4] Reichardt's frustration over her lack of the opportunities afforded to her male counterparts can be heard in a 2011 interview when she says that "the door wasn't open" for her as it was for other first-time directors and their films, such as Kevin Smith's *Clerks* and David O. Russell's *Spanking the Monkey*.[5] These films fit into a male-centric ideal of cinema, while *River of Grass* focuses on a female protagonist and highlights women's concerns and issues.

A FEMALE-CENTERED ROAD MOVIE

River of Grass may be the only road movie whose characters never travel out of their own town. Interlaced with noir, crime thriller, and comedic elements, it keeps audiences guessing, a central feature of Reichardt's mixed-genre film. The road movie, traditionally a very male genre, is turned upside down and inside out by the presentation of a rebellious female variation with little to no violence and almost no real travel. At first glance the plot seems to resemble road movies like *Bonnie and Clyde* (1967) or *Natural Born Killers* (1994)—but Reichardt is playing with male genre conventions to create a strikingly unconventional protagonist in Cozy (Lisa Bowman), who "passively" contradicts all the conventional notions of what Western women should aspire to: marriage, motherhood, and domesticity. This type of protagonist is seen again in Reichardt's fourth feature, *Meek's Cutoff* (2010), an arguably feminist Western with a female protagonist who, like Cozy, steps out of her socially dictated role.

In *River of Grass* audiences are introduced to Cozy, a married mother of three, through her voice-over exposition and continued narration throughout the film. Cozy meets the single and directionless Lee (Larry Fessenden), the film's other main character, at a bar, and they go "on the lam," believing they have accidentally shot and killed a man. Jimmy Rider (Dick Russell) is Cozy's father, who with the help of his crime scene detective co-workers tries to track down Cozy and piece together what caused her disappearance. Reichardt discusses the difficulty of creating a "rebel character" during an age when everyone is encouraged to rebel: "We talked about the idea of updating the rebel character in the context of a road movie. We wondered how the lone rebel, a fixture in every road movie, could exist in the '90s when even the Burger King slogan tells you to 'Break the Rules.'"[6] By switching the gender of the rebel and highlighting female taboos in a traditionally male genre, Reichardt found an alternative formula.

Reichardt has explained that she sees independent filmmaking as a way for underrepresented people to have a voice. *River of Grass*, along with her other films, creates space for topics and behaviors that are taboo for women:

> I think independent cinema is really about representing the part of the population that's not represented through mainstream media. In America we rarely look beyond the middle classes, and I think we're really not the sort of people, as a nation, to talk to about poor people. To me, that's what the heart of alternative art and independent cinema was born from, giving a voice to other parts of the population.[7]

Cozy represents some of the "other parts" of the American population: poor and female. While all the characters in *River of Grass* are poor working class, Cozy represents a mother figure who also deals with post-partum depression and extreme loneliness. In many ways, Cozy's struggles represent Reichardt's own ordeal while making the film. Reichardt suggests the connection between the production and the film's content when discussing the ending, in which Cozy becomes disenchanted enough to shoot Lee: "The film used to have a different ending. The way it ends now is a direct result of my experience in making the film. Cozy gets to play out my fantasy which is what gets her to the other side of all the bullshit—where, by the way, we both find out there's just more bullshit."[8]

Another theme, one that is more subtly explored, is environmentalism and the impact of urban sprawl on lower-class populations. Reichardt's title connects the film to Florida, as it references the Everglades, but her use of a Native American name for the area reminds audiences of its original use, as explained in Cozy's narration:

> Most tourists visit the Miami area for its beaches on the east coast, but if you ever mistakenly get on the Palmetto Expressway and headed west— you'd run right into the Florida Everglades—an area that Indians like to call the river of grass. People used to think this area was uninhabitable but more and more it is becoming civilized. And they say that within two years there will be a shopping center every fifteen miles.[9]

Reichardt's dialogue suggests that this area of Florida is hidden away and that tourists find it by mistake, underscoring how the land, like the people it represents, has been marginalized. The word "civilized" is reminiscent of the missionary work in the American West that ultimately led to a systematic stripping away of the cultural values and traditions of Native American communities. Further developing this connection, Cozy reminds us that the Everglades are slowly turning into retail space, and like the loss of indigenous cultures, the slow degradation of an important environmental habitat will have a global effect. Right before Cozy's explanation, Reichardt juxtaposes a peaceful scene of an African American couple pulling a fish from the water on the bank of the Everglades, and a 180-degree camera turn showing a four-lane Florida highway with cars speeding past. With these two scenes, audiences see the result of an excessive capitalist appetite that ultimately depletes and destroys nature's resources. The following scenes show the extreme measures needed to bend nature to human progress, as Cozy drives by miles of construction sites that look like a moonscape with barren, burnt earth piled high by bulldozers. The final scene in this sequence is a manicured green space, used to divide the highway, with tall palm trees and ball-shaped green bushes. Reichardt is making a comment about her home and how the destruction of a natural resource that helped define it is not only a loss to the environment, but to the lower-working-class population who might have depended on it for sustainability.

While the film illustrates Reichardt's concern for her native environment, she had to be convinced by her producer, Jesse Hartman, to return home to Miami to shoot it. Reichardt and her crew knew that working within the confines of a low budget would prove challenging, but they did not anticipate police interference:

> Miami boasts about being film-friendly. Well, if you're Stallone I'm sure they're plenty friendly. But they don't have a concept of low-budget filmmaking. So there were these constant run-ins with the cops. It was ironic because here we were shooting a film where Cozy and Lee are on the run, and meanwhile the Miami cops actually tried to arrest Lisa Bowman on a daily basis. To be fair she was driving around Dade County waving a prop gun . . . Nineteen days [for the shoot]. On day two they arrested our gaffer and confiscated all of our equipment.[10]

Actors inevitably come with limitations, and Cozy, played by Lisa Bowman, only had seven days to spend on set before heading back to waitress at Two Boots in New York. The silver lining, however, is that this prompted Reichardt to make interesting adjustments to the opening scenes:

> I knew when we were still in Miami that it [seven days with Bowman] wasn't going to be enough. I wanted there to be some sort of a history

in the beginning but I wasn't exactly sure what I was going to do. So I was writing different things and I'd lay them in my voice for the time being . . . I eventually replaced everything with photographs but there is still one piece of Super 8 footage in the opening, the make-out scene . . . Then we shot the hatchet scene here in New York in my friend's apartment.[11]

The year-long search for Cozy was an unconventional aspect of the production of *River of Grass*. Even though Reichardt at first looked for the standard young female lead to play the role, she eventually found that casting an older woman contributed to the realism of the film:

I told her [Bowman] I was looking for a younger version of her for my film, so the next time I saw her she gave me this old head shot she had had taken when she was about nineteen. I right away thought, Wow, that's Cozy, I'll have to find someone just like her. So I carried that photo of Lisa around with me for a year. Then when we were driving down to Florida to do some local casting I started thinking about Cozy being older—closer to my own age, I was twenty-nine at the time. It was an age I could better relate to and it also meant Lisa could play the role.[12]

In addition to casting believable characters, Reichardt put the working-class areas of Miami and its population on screen: "Whenever it was possible we would use real people from each location, like the workers at the bus station or the cashier at the convenience store."[13] Not only did this complement the realistic elements of the film, it was also a practical choice in the context of micro-budget filmmaking. In an interview, Reichardt discusses her debut as a filmmaker and her process: "If you watch *River of Grass* you'll see I haven't quite figured it [filmmaking] out. I didn't know about screenplay structure. I was just breaking down movies I liked on note cards and trying to figure out the rhyme or reason of it."[14] But *River of Grass* is clearly a film that deconstructs, among other things, genre, gender, and film technique. Reichardt might not have been able to label her filmmaking methods when she created it, but many of her scenes, through their content and form, reflect an innate ability to address the female perspective, negate the "male gaze," and offer a feminist counter-cinema.[15]

FEMINIST COUNTER-CINEMA

Laura Mulvey's 1975 article "Visual Pleasure and Narrative Cinema" draws upon psychoanalysis, film, and feminist theory to suggest that the "male gaze"

inherent in classical Hollywood films placed spectators in a voyeuristic position, objectifying and fetishizing women on screen. In an effort to offer an
alternative perspective, Mulvey called for the creation of a counter-cinema.
To achieve this, feminist filmmakers have frequently drawn on 1960s French
New Wave methods such as fragmented and deconstructed narratives. One
goal in feminist counter-cinema is to remind viewers, through self-reflexive
strategies, that they are watching a film, and to offer a feminist alternative to
the mainstream.

While there is no doubt that Mulvey's article transformed film theory, her
ideas created controversy. In her 1983 book *Women and Film: Both Sides of
the Camera*, E. Ann Kaplan comments in reference to Mulvey that "female
characters can possess the look and even make the male character the object of
her gaze, but, being a woman, her desire has no power . . . to own and activate
the gaze, given our language and the structure of the unconscious, is to be in
the 'masculine' position."[16] Kaplan also suggested that because of a patriarchal
social construction, a female look was difficult if not impossible to depict.
Jackie Stacey, in her 1987 article "Desperately Seeking Difference," stated that
"feminist film critics have written the darkest scenario possible for the female
look as being male, masochist or marginal."[17] A handful of feminist critics
agreed with Stacey, including Gaylyn Studlar, who saw the possibility of
female spectator pleasure through Hollywood's female characterization of the
vamp or the femme fatale: "[T]he sexual ambivalence of the vamp . . . allows
for a female homoerotic pleasure that is not exclusively negotiated through the
eyes of men." Studlar argued that "visual pleasure in cinema resembles more
the psychic processes of masochism than of sadism," thus allowing female
viewers to escape the male gaze and "identify with and draw pleasure from the
powerful femme fatale."[18] While Studlar agreed with Stacey that Mulvey had
painted a dark and limited picture for female spectator pleasure, Studlar also
seemed to limit pleasure to specific types of female characters.

In 1991, feminist film theorist Mary Ann Doane contributed the idea of
the female masquerade. Drawing on Mulvey's theories, Doane suggested that
voyeurism naturally creates a barrier or distance: "the female spectator lacks
this necessary distance because she is the image. She is consumed by the image
instead of consuming it."[19] Doane concluded that the only way a woman could
find pleasure in spectatorship was by creating a mask of femininity so she
too could separate herself from the female images on screen; but in doing so,
Doane argued, female spectators fell back into a male gaze, especially in melodrama, since the possibility of "overidentification" leads to "destroying the
distance to the object of desire and turning the active desire of both the female
character and the female spectator into the passive desire. [Therefore] [m]ere
'desire to desire' seems to be, then the only option for women."[20] The debate
about female spectator pleasure continues to be discussed in works by feminist

film theorists such as Claire Johnston, Molly Haskell, bell hooks, and Ruby Rich, who pull away from psychoanalysis and focus on female representation, identity, and perspective. Current theorists have also opened the conversation to include the representation of women of color and a diverse range of sexual orientations, the lack of which was one criticism of early feminist film research.

Kelly Reichardt contributes to the discussion of female spectator pleasure by using feminist counter-cinema techniques to construct female subjectivity, and by featuring female protagonists, highlighting women's issues, and creating scenes that emphasize human connections through relationships rather than actions. These featured relationships are also free of traditional heterosexual romance plots, since the focus in all her films is on working through issues or situations. In Reichardt's films, female spectators are not compelled to "consume" their own image, as Doane argues happens in classical Hollywood films. Instead female spectators look at, identify with, and enjoy a centralized female image working through situations that transcend gender. Reichardt emphasizes gender and gender relationships without creating an overt, didactic feminist agenda as was typical of many 1970s feminist counter-cinema directors. There is no question that her first film, *River of Grass*, fits into a feminist tradition, as it is about breaking barriers and inverting or playing against notions of the male gaze.

In *River of Grass* Reichardt upends traditional filmmaking forms which take away female power and voice, so that they instead highlight the woman as subject. According to feminist Marxist film theorist Christine Gledhill: "Devices such as the close-up or voice-over construct meaning less by what they show or say than by the way they organize the female image into a patriarchal position, or, conversely, offer textual opportunities for resistance."[21] Cozy's voice-over narration in exposition scenes and throughout the film places her in control of the spectator's experience, and as it is not filmed in first person, the voice-over serves to pull the audience back into her consciousness and remind them that she is telling her own story. This organization of "the female image" situates the film within feminist theoretical conversations about realism and antirealism. While the 1970s feminist film theorists called for "realism as the responsible goal of art and entertainment seeking to counteract the false stereotypes of capitalist and patriarchal culture," many socially conscious artists worked toward alternative practices that "espoused a combative antirealism."[22]

Of all Reichardt's features, *River of Grass* is the most experimental and openly counters the patriarchal perspective of traditional cinema with an "alternative practice." Cozy reminds viewers of their voyeurism through shots that feature her direct eye contact, and Reichardt disrupts the narrative through "foregrounding" (a term Peter Wollen explains in his article, "Godard and Counter Cinema: Vent d'est") with still photography, grainy Super 8 film footage,

Figure 3.1 Segment slide in *River of Grass*

and segmented chapters to make "the mechanics of the film/text visible and explicit."[23] *River of Grass* opens with audio of Cozy's expositional voice-over while audiences are shown eight photographs woven in between four moving short segments, one on Super 8. Thirty-three minutes later, viewers are given the first of four unexpected narrative breaks as the scene abruptly cuts to a black screen (Figure 3.1). The only indication that there is a segmenting of the narrative into chapters is that the black screens are numbered one through four, each with increasing bullet holes beside the number. There is no narrative or time-oriented pattern to predict when the segmenting chapter screens will appear, but each is preceded by Ryder's drumbeats. In an effort to explain why a filmmaker like Reichardt would use foregrounding in the way that Godard did, Wollen suggests the director "is looking for a way of expressing negation," and "once the decision is made to consider a film as a process of writing in images, rather than a representation of the world, then it becomes possible to conceive of scratching the film as an erasure, a virtual negation."[24]

By exposing the filmmaking process to her audience through experimentation with "'image-building' as a kind of pictography, in which images are liberated from their role as elements of representation," Reichardt has created the least realistic feature film in her collection.[25] In other words, Wollen points to the issue that image sequences in a film are "the problem of finding an image to signify" an emotion or thought such as oppression. Exposing this process results in a form of metacognition, since the film is acknowledging its image's failure to "signify." Audiences see Reichardt's "pictography" through the still photography in the opening sequence, the extended images of nature, and her decision to use numbered black screen dividers to section off the latter half of the film. As Cozy narrates her taboo desire for a "nice couple in a station wagon to come pick her kids up" and take them away for good, viewers are watching ants crawling on the sidewalk or viewing an abrupt cut to a black screen, witnessing the inability of an image to signify her oppressed state. Although Reichardt moves away from this type of experimental filmmaking almost completely with her next feature, *Old Joy*, the desire to continue producing films that use foregrounding is obvious in two of her short experimental films, *Then, a Year* (2002) and *Travis* (2004).

TABOO TOPICS: POST-PARTUM AND ROLE REVERSALS

In *River of Grass* Reichardt offers alternative views of relationships through gender role reversals and taboo reactions to motherhood, parenting, crime, and heterosexuality. Subverting the male gaze, Reichardt creates a female character who steps outside of socially acceptable boundaries by performing taboo actions. As Judith Butler contends, gender is a social construct that is performed: "[G]ender cannot be understood as a role which either expresses or disguises an interior 'self,' whether that 'self' is conceived as sexed or not."[26] As performance which is performative, gender is an "act," and Cozy is not acting out her socially scripted motherhood role.[27] She is not a traditional or even a socially acceptable mother; she has no problem leaving her two youngest children crying in a playpen while she does cartwheels and stretches in the yard next to them. During a morning scene, breakfast consists of dry Froot Loops in a Tupperware bowl, Coke in a baby bottle, and smoke wafting from Cozy's cigarette; the only parental image during the scene is of Bobby, her husband, holding their middle child in his lap while carefully feeding him baby food. The gender role reversal in parenting is intentional and overt; Cozy smokes and carelessly hands soda to her youngest, she has a full plate of food in front of her, and Bobby is dressed for work, has no food, and lavishes attention on the child in his lap.

Post-partum depression and lack of interest in children from mothers are not topics women frequently discuss openly or admit to publicly. Reichardt's inspiration for Cozy lay in having seen her sister deal with motherhood: "It was partly seeing my sister go through her pregnancy . . . She didn't know if she was ready to give everything else up. But as soon as she'd express any of that, whoever was around would immediately shush her up, as if it were sacrilegious to even think that way—'Of course you'll love giving everything up!'"[28] If the breakfast images are not enough to convey the gender role reversals, Cozy's voice-over says it all:

I've heard it said that the mother-child bond begins at birth; for me this never occurred. And on some days, I'd sit at my window for hours, just waiting for a nice couple in a big station wagon to come and take these kids away. Too much daydreaming left me blue, so while Bobby worked day and night, I stayed home and tried to make the best of my time.

After Cozy narrates the breakfast scene, the camera cuts to her doing cart-wheels in her living room that evening and when finished, she takes three bows to her pretend audience with a half-smile simulating pride in her performance. The scene feels unnaturally extended (as many in the film do when Reichardt is experimenting with "slow cinema" techniques), but it allows spectators to fully take in Cozy's lonely and unfulfilled life as a mother. She has what Betty Friedan, in her foundational work *The Feminine Mystique*, would call "the problem that has no name."[29] While Cozy does not belong to the suburban housewife socioeconomic category that fits many of the women Friedan inter-viewed, she is clearly performing her role as a mother with little joy or interest. Cozy acts her parts as girl, woman, and mother, but they do not suit her, and depression ensues. When she leaves her home to have a beer at a local bar, a stationary camera centers on her sleeping infant while she walks into the frame, around the baby, and quietly tiptoes out the front door. Spectators realize that she is leaving her small child alone at home as the door closes and the camera lingers on the angelic sleeping baby. While this scene is intentionally shock-ing and (as Todd Haynes points out in an interview) risky, since viewers may dislike Cozy for her parental decisions, it highlights a motif concerning the lack of parental models and a theme of childhood neglect. In her film Reichardt questions the idea of "mother blaming" by considering maternal influence. Earlier in the film, Cozy's concern about her daughter's future and her own mother's influence echoes this theme: "They say that the apple doesn't fall far from the tree . . . would my daughter grow up only to wear my shoes; did my mother's life create my destiny?"

While Cozy's narration at the beginning of the film states that her mother left the family at an early age, it is not until Lee and Cozy escape to a hotel and begin to discuss their childhoods that audiences learn more about her role models for parenting. Cozy describes the fight she heard between her parents when, on vacation, they stopped at an RV park in their camper van: "I could hear her outside yelling, 'Jimmy, this is the devil. I want you to come out and play with me.' And my dad yelled out, 'And this is God and if you don't just shut up I'm going to strike you dead.' I rode the whole way home in the back of the camper, not even knowing my mom wasn't with us." After her mother leaves, presumably, Cozy's father transforms into a very maternal figure, adopting abandoned animals from his crime scenes, insisting she attend a Catholic church, and making her go to weekly confessionals. In other words, the stereotypical gender roles reverse, with the mother leaving the family and the father adopting religion to cope with raising a daughter: "Dad was never a religious man but after Mom left, he decided to raise me Catholic." Lee adds to the theme of parental tales a few scenes later by stating that his father married his mother for a second time and on their honeymoon stood up, drink in hand, fully dressed, and drowned himself in the ocean. His mother subsequently supported them by marrying different men, but she has recently been in a "slump," or they would not be living at his grandmother's home. In addition to creating characters who perform the opposing gender's socially dictated roles, Reichardt rigorously excludes sentimentality from her script and character depiction. While this lack of sentimentality is common to all her films and is arguably an auteur quality, she explains in discussing *River of Grass*: "I had planned on having it so that whenever any character would open up and reveal something of themselves, nobody would be listening and that got carried over—really every intimate moment was spent alone."[30]

POWERLESS MEN

Reichardt's feminist counter-cinema is characterized not only by gender role reversals but by the rejection of traditional stereotypes and the creation of powerless men. This lack of internal or external power fills the content of her film while she emphasizes it, and in the process negates the male gaze through her fragmented shots, framing, lack of male eyeline matches, and female-oriented point of view shots. Throughout the film, Bobby, Ryder, Ryder's co-workers, and Lee repeatedly illustrate an emotional or physical inadequacy that is underscored by their fragmented representation. Audiences see only parts of the male characters' bodies, as when Lee is driving, cut in half by doorframes and bar counters, or shown getting a tattoo on a body part. Ryder is also halved by bar counters, but mainly by his drum set; and Bobby is seen only three times, but never occupying the whole screen. When their bodies are seen in their entirety it is from a distance, with either Cozy's cartwheels or traffic separating viewers from the male characters. Even minor characters such as Ryder's fellow crime scene detectives seem inert as they follow Cozy and Lee's trail with no substantial progress, even though Lee, Ryder, and a fellow detective cross paths in a local record store. As if to emphasize this point, Reichardt has Ryder's co-worker pull Cozy and her children over onto the side of the road only to "pass the time" and casually discuss family issues. While this scene is seemingly irrelevant to the plot, it serves as another indication that the men in *River of Grass* are stagnant and powerless.

While Bobby holds down two jobs and seems to be a responsible parent, he is simultaneously characterized as a person with no aspirations who is easily

Figure 3.2 Bobby holding the baby

manipulated by his wife. Bobby seems to have chosen to live in a loveless marriage and insisted on having three children even though there was obviously no desire to do so from his partner. In a shared scene between Ryder and Bobby after they discover Cozy has left the children at home alone, Ryder asks if they had a fight, and Bobby replies: "Yeah I guess, more like an argument really" (Figure 3.2). Ryder's quizzical look at Bobby expresses what the audience is thinking—with only five lines in the entire film, Bobby has nothing important to share. Both men's bodies are fragmented as each holds an infant and the camera virtually renders Bobby invisible. Bobby could easily fit into the mother or wife role of a classical Hollywood melodrama.

Ryder is featured on screen much more than Bobby, but he still exudes defeat. One example of his powerlessness is when he takes a woman home from a bar, at her suggestion; the next morning, instead of talking with her, he plays drums while she puts on make-up. Audiences are already aware of Ryder's lack of power; during his introductory scene, he fails to stop a bar robbery because he is unable to find his gun or catch up with the criminal during a chase. When he stops in his chase and finds no gun in his holster, the camera pans down to show the ocean waves breaking over his feet; Ryder is literally and metaphorically washed up before the film even begins.

Lee consistently proves his inability to progress in life, and Reichardt's cinematic techniques emphasize this. All of Lee's attempts to break the law fail: finding rather than stealing a gun; being unable to initiate a robbery and getting punched in the process; failing to run through a tollbooth stop, or to

Figure 3.3 Lee at the tollbooth with an officer

resist questioning from a condescending state patrol officer (Figure 3.3). In all three of these scene sequences Lee is permitted only two point of view shots or eyeline matches, resulting in a distancing effect for spectators. The camera is purposely held away from Lee so that audiences view him objectively; or often, as in the patrol officer scene, they view the events from Cozy's position. Lee's ineffectuality is illustrated when he is locked out of his grandmother's house. Not only is he emasculated by having to live with his mother at his grandmother's home and abide by their rules, he is unsuccessful at getting back into her house when she changes the locks—which gives her time to throw out all of his belongings. Audiences watch from a low-angle camera shot as he beats on her door and finally gives up. Lee is rendered homeless within half a day and, with no prospects or desire to move forward, he joins the other impotent men in Reichardt's film; in fact, rather than just joining the other male characters in their ineffectuality, he leads them. During the film's climax Cozy, driving with gun in hand, shoots Lee while he is in mid-sentence. Cozy is framed in the center of the shot until after she uses the gun, and then the camera cuts to show her shutting the door after she pushes Lee's dead body out of the car (Figure 3.4). Not only does Reichardt's framing place Cozy in a position of power, but Lee is heard and framed in ways that suggest he is, and always has been, a peripheral character.

River of Grass provides alternatives to a heterosexual romance and subverts audience expectations not only of the leads' relationship but also of female behavior and desire. In many reviews Lee and Cozy are compared to Bonnie

Figure 3.4 Cozy shoots Lee

and Clyde or labeled as "expectant lovers" who flirt at first sight, but on closer inspection these descriptions are far from accurate. *River of Grass* does not fit into any romanticized version of a road movie or noir, because Cozy only exudes self-interest. She is not smitten by, does not seek approval or attention from, and is not dominated by any male figure. Cozy does trade her autonomy for human connection when she leaves with Lee, however, and Reichardt uses this to deconstruct the road movie genre. Cozy and Lee's inability to break through their individual loneliness and make emotional connections during their time together causes them to stagnate in Broward County without any hope of achieving real movement or progression in their situation—one convention of the road movie genre. Reviewer David Liu makes an effective comparison when he says, "Reichardt's protagonists . . . are Bonnie and Clyde for the slacker generation, imperfectly embodying the latter's particular brand of pop-culture nihilism: 'If we weren't killers, we weren't anything.'"[31] That "anything" includes any type of romantic or sexual relationship. Cozy never at any point seems taken with Lee. In their initial conversation, Lee attempts to be assertive by asking Cozy if he can buy her a drink, but he botches it in a moment of insecurity, mumbling that the purpose of his gesture is to apologize for nearly hitting her with his car. Lee seems to want to make connections and build relationships with others, but like the other men in the film, he is completely incapable. The next scene shows them sitting together while Cozy dances in her seat, drinking a free beer, and barely noticing Lee next to her. In an attempt to impress her Lee empties the contents of his wallet in a grandiose style, and Cozy asks, "Is that supposed to impress me?" In his next attempt he displays his arm, emblazoned with a recent "Mom" tattoo, and she points to a picture of his mother from the wallet and says, "Mom? We already have Mom here." Lee represents the Freudian theory that men look for mother figures in their relationships; Cozy not only flatly rejects this role but also finds it comical, as her laughing response indicates. The evening at the bar ends with both of them sitting staring forward with no interaction, lost in reflection on their unhappy and limiting lives.

LIMINAL EXISTENCE

Being in "limbo" becomes a theme for all the characters in the film as none advance or even hope to in any way, whether socioeconomic, parental, physical, or emotional. It is during the bar scene that Lee describes himself as being in limbo and Cozy replies, "Limbo—that sounds nice." Reichardt creates a visual limbo for Cozy in two scenes where she appears to be balancing between planes of existence. The first is at the opening of the film when Cozy is half submerged in her bathtub, floating silently and still. Spectators are confronted with her staring back at them, aware of her audience (Figure 3.5). Her voice-over narration stings, reminding viewers they are voyeurs looking at a living, feeling woman during what should be a private moment. In her voice-over Cozy contemplates the violent history of the previous owner of her home, a

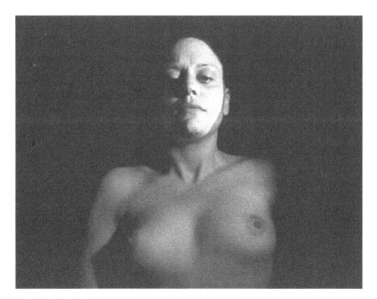

Figure 3.5 Cozy in the bathtub

woman who killed her husband: "I often thought about this woman and won-dered what made her act so violently. I guess it wasn't any one big thing but a lot of little things that just grow deeper and deeper under our skin." The combination of Cozy's direct eye contact with the camera, the suggestion of unhappiness in women's lives, the word "skin," and her naked body floating in limbo creates a cyclical mini-narrative about women's lives, all before the film feels like it has begun.

One thread in that narrative returns to Reichardt's use of feminist counter-cinema and rejection of the male gaze. Cozy stares back at the camera as it invades her private space, with an accusatory wrinkle in her brow and flat but knowing eyes. While viewers of both genders squirm in their seats, having been caught "looking," male spectators find reproach while female spectators may find connection. A second thread entails a foreshadowing of violence, unhappiness, and limbo. In the scenes directly before Cozy floats in her tub, spectators watch a woman drag her dead husband to the shower (presumably in Cozy's bathroom) and violently chop him to pieces. With a low-angle shot, the camera stays focused on the blood-splattered wife, never moving to show her victim, as she wipes tears from her face and cries between each blow, her distress obvious. This grisly scene represents action and movement, which the characters in the film notably lack. While many films portray extreme vio-lence, producing desensitization, spectators rarely see women performing such bloody and vicious acts. The woman's actions foreshadow the ending of the film, when Cozy too turns her anger outward instead of inward. A third thread revolves around images of the female body: Cozy's body is realistic rather than a typical Hollywood representation of symmetrical beauty, and in being so it is intentionally disarming, as Reichardt explains:

> To me, it gives the audience a break, especially if you're a woman—to see a woman in a lead role with a body and a face that you can relate to. The window of what makes a woman beautiful seems to get smaller and smaller. A straight woman doesn't see a lot of other naked women except for what's on TV or in the movies. And it's a little freaky when seemingly everybody else's breasts are getting perkier as they get older.[32]

All three of these threads connect during Cozy's tub scene and as it fades to black, purposely leaving space before the opening credits, spectators have a moment to fully contemplate the sequence of female-centered images and issues Reichardt has highlighted before the opening credits.

The second scene that illustrates Cozy's suspended state is when Lee con-vinces her to leave the bar with him and swim in his former high school teacher's pool. Unannounced to its owner, Cozy dives into the pool com-pletely clothed and floats on her back, making water angels. Watching from

Figure 3.6 Cozy in the pool

a bird's-eye perspective, spectators are not confronted with their voyeurism because Cozy is in a public location, fully clothed, and vigorously moving, in contrast to the bathtub scene (Figure 3.6). Water allows Cozy to physically float between two spaces and reflects her liminal existence as a wife, mother, and woman. In addition to water, pregnancy denotes a biological transitional state, and by representing Cozy's body in multiple forms of suspension Reichardt is conveying the liminal quality of the female experience, especially as defined under patriarchy. As if underscoring this point, while Cozy floats, absorbed in the moment, the scene abruptly switches to her home, reminding spectators of her motherhood as her father holds one infant and Bobby paces with another, while they work to figure out Cozy's motives for leaving. Bobby suggests their argument was the impetus, but viewers know Cozy was neither angry nor in a hurry when she dressed and left for her night out. Anger implies emotional connection to others, and while Cozy feels nothing for anyone else in the film, she does at least recognize her desire for something different.

In representing female-owned desire with no masculine impetus, Cozy is rare in the world of film, and exemplifies Reichardt's subversive characterization. Some critics, however, argue that the pool scenes illustrate that Cozy is less emotionally disconnected from Lee than she is from other parts of her life. J. J. Murphy suggests that there is a hint of sexual intimacy between the two: "As Cozy climbs out of the water and positions herself between Lee's legs, we expect him to kiss her as he leans forward, but, in a sexually-loaded gesture, Lee thrusts the pistol into her hands."[33] Cozy maintains control throughout the narrative. She swims to Lee simply because she wants to hold the gun, and not because she wants to make a connection, as asserted by Reichardt: "The gun in that scene is the real object of desire—at least it is for Cozy."[34] Once Lee's friend Doug discovers the gun on the street, it becomes a character. Each time the gun appears the viewer sucks in a breath, wonders whether it is loaded, and crosses fingers as the characters carelessly wave it around and point it at friends or family. The gun is central to the plot, but it is also central to Cozy's desire, in that it represents the power to create change and produce movement. In the final scenes of the film Cozy never lets the gun out of her sight, and even drives holding it against the steering wheel. As Lee narrates a possible life together, unknowingly describing her current situation with Bobby, Cozy becomes more and more frustrated. Lee embodies stagnation and the gun is Cozy's ticket to freedom, so whether premeditated or not, Cozy's decision to shoot Lee with the gun—a traditionally masculine symbol—illustrates a resistance to and a breaking away from the patriarchal status quo.

Because *River of Grass* was Reichardt's first feature it allowed room for experimentation with style and technique, and in her next three features audiences and critics can see a refinement of those cinematic choices. While she stays away from overtly experimental elements in her features, confining them to her shorts, she continues to make use of minimalism and realism through source sound, available light, on-location shooting, and dialogue-driven scenes. She also continues to play with genre by intermixing the road movie with buddy movie elements in *Old Joy* and *Wendy and Lucy*, and then by creating a feminist Western in *Meek's Cutoff*. What becomes more pronounced through each film, seeded in *River of Grass*, is her use of slow cinematic techniques. Reichardt's extensive use of long takes, subdued visual schemes that require spectators to be engaged, and an emphasis on the everyday can be seen to varying degrees in all her features, but culminate in *Meek's Cutoff*. She gravitates toward neorealism and "slow cinema" techniques that align her more broadly with art cinema and international avant-garde, and in a strategic career move, she distances herself from overtly feminist styles while offering a contribution to feminist counter-cinema. Reichardt's first feature might not have opened the doors to Hollywood funding opportunities, but it does represent the beginnings of an auteur.

NOTES

1. Anne Thompson, "Meek's Cutoff: Professor Kelly Reichardt's Filmmaking 101 Primer," *IndieWire*, 21 April 2011.
2. Reichardt quoted in Mike Plante, "Kelly Reichardt: Meet the Artist," *Sundance Film Festival*, 2011.

3. Jesse Hawthorne Ficks, "Northwest Passage: Kelly Reichardt on 'Meek's Cutoff,'" *San Francisco Bay Guardian Online*, 3 May 2011, <http://48hills.org/sfbgarchive/2011/05/03/northwest-passage-kelly-reichardt-meeks-cutoff/> (accessed 20 September 2017).

4. "*River of Grass* (1994): Awards," *Internet Movie Database*, <http://www.imdb.com/title/tt0110998/awards?ref_=tt_ql_op_1> (accessed 20 September 2017).

5. Karina Longworth, "Kelly Reichardt Explains 'Meek's Cutoff,' Her Latest Road Movie," *San Francisco Weekly*, 4 May 2011, <https://archives.sfweekly.com/sanfrancisco/kelly-reichardt-explains-meeks-cutoff-her-latest-road-movie/Content?oid=2181363> (accessed 20 September 2017).

6. Reichardt quoted in Todd Haynes, "Kelly Reichardt," *Bomb* 53 (1995), <http://bombmagazine.org/article/1891/kelly-reichardt> (accessed 20 September 2017).

7. Reichardt quoted in Adam Woodward, "Kelly Reichardt Review," *Little White Lies* (2011).

8. Reichardt quoted in Haynes, "Kelly Reichardt."

9. Ibid.

10. Ibid.

11. Ibid.

12. Ibid.

13. Ibid.

14. Reichardt quoted in Plante, "Meet the Artist."

15. Ibid.

16. E. Ann Kaplan, *Women and Film: Both Sides of the Camera* (New York: Methuen, 1988), p. 30.

17. Pam Cook (ed.), *The Cinema Book*, 3rd edn. (London: British Film Institute, 2007), p. 495.

18. Gaylyn Studlar quoted in Cook, *The Cinema Book*, p. 495.

19. Cook, *The Cinema Book*, p. 495.

20. Ibid.

21. Christine Gledhill, "Image and Voice: Approaches to Marxist-Feminist Film Criticism," in Diane Carson et al. (eds.), *Multiple Voices in Feminist Film Criticism* (Minneapolis: Minnesota University Press, 1994), p. 114.

22. Ibid. p. 115.

23. Peter Wollen, "Godard and Counter Cinema: *Vent d'Est*," in Leo Braudy and Marshall Cohen (eds.), *Film Theory and Criticism*, 5th edn. (New York: Oxford University Press, 1999), p. 501.

24. Ibid. p. 502.

25. Ibid.

26. Judith Butler, "Performative Acts and Gender Constitution: An Essay in Phenomenology and Feminist Theory," in Amelia Jones (ed.), *The Feminism and Visual Culture Reader* (London: Routledge, 2003), p. 279.

27. Ibid.

28. Reichardt quoted in Haynes, "Kelly Reichardt."

29. Betty Friedan, *The Feminine Mystique* (New York: W. W. Norton & Company, 1963), p. 43.

30. Reichardt quoted in Haynes, "Kelly Reichardt."

31. David Liu, "It Takes a Train to Cry: The Cinema of Kelly Reichardt," *Kino Obscura*, 19 November 2010, <http://kino-obscura.com/post/1619587333/it-takes-a-train-to-cry> (accessed 20 September 2017).

32. Reichardt quoted in Haynes, "Kelly Reichardt."
33. J. J. Murphy, "*River of Grass*" (blog post), 22 July 2009, <http://www.jjmurphyfilm. com/blog/2009/07/22/river-of-grass/> (accessed 20 September 2017).
34. Reichardt quoted in Haynes, "Kelly Reichardt."

CHAPTER 4

Growth: *Ode*; *Then, a Year*; and *Travis*

I had this great epiphany when I was standing in a field with friends
making an art project [*Ode*] . . . how can I sustain something like this?—
Kelly Reichardt[1]

Very little scholarly work has been written about Reichardt's short films,
especially those no longer in circulation. Using documentary-style realism
mixed with audio of news footage, Reichardt asks difficult questions about social
values. In all her films she comments on social and political issues, but her shorts
differ in that she creates a kinetic experience so audiences engage in "haptic
viewing." In her book *The Skin of the Film* Laura Marks suggests this type of
looking happens when viewers' eyes "move over the surface of [their] object
rather than . . . plunge into illusionistic depth" in an effort to "discern texture."[2]
Reichardt achieves a haptic sensibility most notably via form, using 16mm or
Super 8 film, but also through content, since haptic visuality calls for "forcing
the viewer to contemplate the image itself instead of being pulled into narrative,"[3] an experience she creates in every film through pacing and tempo. All
three short films are connected through this haptic looking as well as through
themes of injustice and loss; and all contain elements of feminist ideology, highlighting a mixture of social and cultural tensions pulled from the headlines.
Ode (1999), a Super 8 adaptation of a Herman Raucher novel made popular by
Bobbie Gentry's song "Ode to Billie Joe," is set in the rural South and follows
an adolescent boy's struggle with his sexuality, ending in suicide. *Then, a Year*
(2001) is a collage of images overlaid with multiple voices discussing real-life
news stories: the well-known statutory rape case perpetrated by Mary Kay
Letourneau, and the murder of a woman by her husband. *Travis* (2004) is based
on a National Public Radio interview with a mother struggling to understand

the loss of her son during the Iraq War. While Reichardt is more experimental in *Then, a Year* and *Travis*, the use of documentary style in all of her early films influences the later narrative features as she explores social and cultural issues.

Typically for Reichardt, the small crews of her shorts were made up of people she had previously worked with. From *River of Grass* Reichardt recruited Lisa Bowman, who played Cozy, as the female voice-over for *Then, a Year*. She also enlisted *River of Grass* actor/editor Larry Fessenden's production company, Glass Eye Pix, for *Ode* and *Then, a Year*. Smokey Hormel's musical talent was also utilized in *Then, a Year*, and Reichardt went on to use him in several of her features, most notably *Wendy and Lucy* (2008). Todd Haynes is a constant entity, showing up in all Reichardt film credits mainly as an executive producer, but he also drew the DVD cover for *Ode* and contributed the roses used in *Then, a Year*. Susan Stover, who produced *Ode*, also assisted with *Then, a Year*. The last short of the trio, *Travis*, was supported by the Wexner Center Media Arts Program at Ohio State University, an artist residency program Reichardt would later utilize for *Certain Women* (2016). With her first feature and subsequent shorts, Reichardt built a knowledgable and talented network of crew who would also be involved in her feature films.

Each of the three shorts contributed uniquely to her growth as a filmmaker. In multiple interviews Reichardt credits *Ode*, the only narrative short, for renewing her joy in feature filmmaking after the twelve-year hiatus between *River of Grass* and *Old Joy*. The other two shorts, both experimental, are exercises in synthesizing audio with visuals to generate uncomfortable emotional responses. *Then, a Year* keeps viewers on edge with a growing sense of dread, and *Travis* is made heart-wrenching by the sorrow and frustration evident in the voice-over. All three shorts are early manifestations of Reichardt's work with slow cinematic techniques in addition to the indirect address of social justice and equality concerns audiences see in her features. What seems to be missing from her shorts, as opposed to the features, is the emphasis on environmental concerns. *Ode* and *Then, a Year* are either set in or highlight nature, but neither have scenes that make a statement about human mismanagement of the environment as directly as do Reichardt's features. However, she does not shy away from discussing social injustice; her depiction of humanity and its issues is honest, clear, and refreshingly transparent, even if her style is not. It is through her use of form, not just content, that Reichardt evokes strong emotional responses and keeps viewers thinking long after the final credits.

ODE (1999)

In interviews Reichardt has suggested that *Ode* helped reignite her artistic drive after she failed to acquire funding for a second feature. In many ways, scaling back allowed her more freedom: "With the next films I made, *Ode* and the short [*Then, a Year*], both of which I was shooting and editing, there was time to learn a lot about filmmaking where there wasn't so much at risk."[4] Reichardt may not have risked much financially, but if the film had received a wider release its subject matter could have caused controversy. Released on the film festival circuit in 1999, *Ode* is an honest depiction of youthful sexuality highlighting the confusion, frustration, and epiphanies teenagers experience as they navigate new emotions. The twist is that while viewers might expect a conventional teenage coming-of-age story—"boy meets girl," with a teenage boy pressuring a girl to have sex—instead the film offers "boy meets boy and then rejects girl."

Ode is a framed story, beginning with the fifteen-year-old Bobbie Lee walking home from First Baptist School and learning that her ex-boyfriend, Billie Joe McAllister, has died by suicide. In disbelief, she leans against a tree and viewers watch the following forty-eight minutes through a mix of objective and subjective shots, before circling back to relive the opening scene. As in *River of Grass*, Reichardt gives the work some experimental qualities by shooting in grainy Super 8, using handheld cameras, and blurring images. At one point, after the two teenagers share a kiss, Bobbie Lee races off on her bike and the camera, as if mounted on the bike, mimics her excitement and the upbeat music by scrambling the image through extreme bouncing. Reichardt is working with haptic visuality, since to apply Laura Marks's concepts, the film *Ode* creates experiences that "privilege the material presence of the image."[5] In this case "[t]he eyes themselves function like organs of touch,"[6] so we are transported onto the bike and "touch" or feel the bumpy field. In the following scenes Bobbie Lee is lying on her bed practice-kissing her doll, Benjamin, and the camera again functions as "haptic looking . . . moving over the surface . . . to discern texture"[7] by lightly tracing her body as it pans from her feet to her head.

As the narrative unfolds, the tension between rebellious youth and strict dogmatic religion moves to the surface. Billie Joe quits his religious school, the only school that would readmit him in the region, claiming fault with the school uniform. In reality he disagrees with the school's teachings, stating that an affiliated group, the Young Life youth organization, has "fire and brimstone" preaching on its website, and initiates a discussion about what constitutes a sin. While Billie Joe explores his sexuality both with a teen boy he meets at a fair and with Bobbie Lee, the real message seems to be about the intolerance of religion and the impact on LGBT youth. When Billie Joe is unable to have sex with Bobbie Lee and confesses he has been hiding in the woods for three days since his encounter at the fair, viewers are witness to a strikingly honest and open conversation. It is a dialogue that could not happen within the religious confines the two are living inside, suggesting a reason why Reichardt

Figure 4.1 Billie Joe and Bobbie Lee in the woods

sets almost the entire film out of doors in natural surroundings. Not only does Billie Joe discuss his desires and lack thereof, he also reassures Bobbie Lee that "It's not us. It's not you. You are fine, beautiful, normal" (Figure 4.1). The last word, "normal," seems to sting both of them, but Billie Joe quickly references typical masculinity norms, saying, "If I'm really a man I need to face up to things," suggesting that those norms could be what drives him to take his own life. Instead of having Bobbie Lee leave the scene, Reichardt keeps her involved in the discussion, and instead of backing away from a sexual encounter she expresses her desire to continue, saying, "I thought when I got my clothes taken off I'd be a woman before they were put back on." Obviously at a stalemate, the two stare at each other, Billie Joe clothed and ready to run into the woods while Bobbie Lee is still half dressed, unmoving. Billie Joe finishes the scene looking at Bobbie Lee and announcing that instead of a woman, she is "nothing but a bruised girl." As if handing the focus back to her, Reichardt conveys to viewers that Bobbie Lee feels metaphorically bruised by all parts of her life. Reichardt captures the teenage struggle for identity and self-acceptance in an oppressive system, while highlighting the dangers that system poses through Billie Joe's death.

As in many of her films, Reichardt is exploring the tension between insiders and outsiders. Bobbie Lee's father is the preacher at First Baptist Church, making her family insiders, while Billie Joe's parents are divorced and he is seen breaking every ideological rule associated with the church's teachings. Many of Reichardt's characters can be categorized as social "outsiders," but

Billie Joe stands out in that he ends his own life owing to a lack of support, education, and role models. The social message in *Ode* resonates more strongly with a contemporary audience than it might have done in 1999, as LGBT civil rights have since gained more ground. Apart from its message, *Ode* seems to be Reichardt's "turning point" film, since she plays with experimental qualities but keeps plot central in comparison to her other shorts. *Ode* foreshadows her ultimate move toward narrative features, but it will only come after she hones her minimalist approach and expresses her artistic freedom through two experimental shorts.

THEN, A YEAR (2001)

The opening of *Then, a Year* (2001) feels like a David Lynch film, since its first impressions and expectations are deceiving. For the full fourteen minutes spectators are shown idyllic images that contrast with the sounds they hear. Spanning from waterfalls and green, leafy trees swaying in the wind to suburbia and household objects, Reichardt contrasts nature with man-made objects and overlays these images with a cacophony of sounds (Figure 4.2). The music, a mix of slow piano and eerie, melancholy whirling, adds a mysterious depth, while at the same time multiple voice-overs narrate broken storylines. Reichardt overlaps cases of domestic abuse and murder, referencing serial killer Jim Hicks as well as Mary Kay Letourneau's statutory rape

Figure 4.2 Waterfall in *Then, a Year*

case.[8] Letourneau was a Seattle middle-school teacher who, following a highly publicized criminal trial in 1997, was sentenced to a seven-year jail term after a sex scandal resulted in her having two children with one of her students.[9] A love letter to the then twelve-year-old student was discovered by Letourneau's husband, confirming the relationship and prompting the beginning of legal action.[10] Lines from Letourneau's letter are read throughout Reichardt's film, but the majority of the narration comes from the television show *Cold Case Files*, pulled from an episode featuring the case against Jim Hicks. Hicks was sentenced to life in prison in 2000 for killing three women, the first of whom was his wife, Jennie Hicks, referenced in the film by name.[11]

Without prior knowledge of these two cases, viewers might conclude from the audio that the film revolves around interviews about a domestic abuse case involving an affair, ending in a jealous husband abusing or murdering his wife. By including Letourneau's case, Reichardt is avoiding the woman as victim stereotype; instead she complicates the message by offering two seemingly different criminal cases, and asks viewers to draw conclusions. Through the use of audio clips, Reichardt's editing sends a message about TV crime shows that profit from tragedy. By splicing together decontextualized, clichéd comments that seem nonsensical and ridiculous (such as "Not only who-done-it, so to speak, but why they done it, so to speak") the film confronts media that thrives on violent crime which victimizes women. American television in the 1990s capitalized on audiences' seemingly unquenchable thirst for documentary- and reality-style crime shows, and in essence reinforced linear and predictable plot structures. These expectations might be reflected in moviegoers' box-office choices as well. Upending viewer expectation, Reichardt's form and content keeps them guessing with no closure.

Then, a Year is filmed on Super 8, and its grainy look creates a textured cinematic quality. The camera never settles on one object for long, and the audio drives the spectators' search for narrative meaning. In perhaps the most tactile or haptic moment of the short film Reichardt creates a series of audience POV shots, allowing viewers to feel as if they are descending a staircase (Figure 4.3). In the vein of virtual reality, the descent is so visceral that viewers temporarily lose track of piecing the narrative together and simply exist within the technical aspect of getting down the stairs without falling. The haptic quality is experienced best as viewers skip down the green-carpeted steps: "The haptic image connects directly to sense perception . . . [and] can bring us to the direct experience of time *through* the body . . . it encourages a bodily relationship between the viewer and the image."[12] Lost in the perfect combination of audio and visual sensations, the handheld camera shakes with each quick step, peering down as if trying not to fall while viewers hear the crunch of stiff carpet.

Aside from the quick stair descent, black-and-white images of suburbia drift past the frame, filmed from a slow-moving vehicle; color images of birds

Figure 4.3 POV shot descending a staircase

on street wires fill the grainy scenes, and we hear ominous screams, some clearly from a woman but others, on closer inspection, from children at a playground (Figure 4.4). While many of the images are traditionally associated with lovers—paths though wooded forests, ducks floating in a city park, rumpled bedsheets and roses—the music keeps viewers uncomfortable. The romantic wooded paths turn into a reminder that Jim Hicks buried two of his victims in the Maine woods; the rumpled white sheets are associated with Letourneau's love letter pleading with her student to stay quiet about their relationship, asking him to give "a life and death promise that you can never tell about us—not even a kiss can be told." As Reichardt pans over innocent images of teddy bears, vases and rose clippers, she is playing with viewers' expectations. She connects predator and victim with her crime documentary voice-overs, but also with images such as that of a black cat lazily licking his mouth and then quietly stalking prey in a field. Reichardt seems to be saying that predators require secrets and silence, as was the case in both of these criminal cases. The title comes at the end of the film, when the TV crime show host says "Then, a year," and dramatic music swells as if to cue a commercial break. Throughout the film, the voice-overs tend toward the theatrical, stating sensational evidence or interview soundbites, but never answering questions or offering a complete narrative. Much like Reichardt's feature films, *Then, a Year* seems designed to generate questions, giving viewers time to meditate on difficult themes that society tends to be uncomfortable addressing.

Figure 4.4 Images of blurry suburbia from a moving car

TRAVIS (2004)

Travis was inspired by a National Public Radio (NPR) interview with a mother who had lost her son during the Iraq War. The last of the three shorts, it came four years after *Then, a Year* and is Reichardt's only publicly available short film. *Then, a Year* and *Travis* are Reichardt's most experimental projects. While her features do have experimental qualities (*River of Grass* dabbles in found footage and 2016's *Certain Women* is broken up into episodes), Reichardt justifies why only these two works are purely experimental: "Narrative is easier for me. I'm much more of a narrative brain. It takes so much effort for me to throw narrative away—it always comes sneaking back in."[13] *Travis* is the culmination of minimalism in both form and content at this point in her career, since with each film leading up to *Travis*, feature or short, she gradually cuts back on dialogue, visuals, and audio. Reichardt narrows to one storyline, a mother mourning her son's death, and one repeated, out-of-focus image, a child's moving figure in the grass, to create an emotionally wrenching but universal story of loss. She selects several phrases from the NPR interview and repeats them, varying the order, during the eleven-minute short. She credits Ira Kaplan, guitarist for Yo La Tengo, the group used in *Old Joy*'s (2006) soundtrack, for the ominous guitar melody, and a few others for Super 8 transfers and editing/sound mixing; but of all her work, this film has the fewest contributors by far. When Reichardt returns to feature filmmaking the political implications within her narratives are still very visible, and the influences of *Travis*, such as the minimalistic script and storyline, can be seen in *Old Joy*, as compared to *River of Grass* or even *Ode*.

Using audio from the NPR interview, Reichardt arranges the spoken narrative about the day the mother learned of her son's death: "No, there's no reason that you'd have to tell me, because there is only one reason you'd come." With only a blurry screen to view, audiences picture officers walking to her front door, as portrayed in so many films, hats in hands with grim faces, to announce her son's death. As with radio, Reichardt relies on her audiences' ability to create images around the audio, depending on active engagement. In fact, the long pauses and irregular patterns help create space for spectators to reflect and meditate, a cinematic quality found in all her films. The most intimate phrases uttered by the mother might be in her retelling of a discussion she had with her son before he was deployed. The film begins with the attention-grabbing audio, "Oh my God. Oh my God," and then, multiple times, viewers hear, "You have to swear to me, swear to me that nothing will happen—I have to truly believe that," indicating that she asked her son to promise he would return home. It is not until ten minutes and forty seconds into the film, the very last phrase spoken, that she adds her imaginings about his thoughts right before his death: "And I just pictured, just pictured, one moment that he knew for just a second—Oh shit mom, I'm so sorry—I know I promised." Immediately after this, the title and credits end the film and the spell Reichardt has cast slowly dissolves, leaving viewers to live a mother's sorrow.

The Iraq War began in March 2003, and with it the American government's search for weapons of mass destruction hidden inside Iraq. These weapons were never found, but the anticipated seizure of them was used as the impetus for invading Iraq. While *Travis* is one mother's reflection about the death of her son, she speaks in dualities, referring to American popular sentiment rationalizing the invasion, saying, "We went in on the premise that that's what it was." Reichardt captures universal feelings of grief and disillusionment with war, and at the same time communicates a very personal story of loss. The film's minimalist audio track subtly reminds viewers that the rationale behind going to war was never confirmed. The phrase "I believe it had to do with dollars and cents" suggests the mother believes, not unlike many Americans at the time, that the war was really about securing rights to oil in the region. This sentiment is somewhat buried, spoken for the first time at six minutes, and the clearest condemnation of the war is spoken at eight minutes: "Now the war is such a mess." As opposed to many Hollywood films that glorify wartime violence, Reichardt creates empathy via a mother's grieving process in an effort to condemn war. *Travis* is a tribute to those who have lost their lives in war, but it also reminds viewers of the sacrifices endured by families at the hands of government.

Reichardt experiments with voice in her shorts in interesting and complex ways, and all of these techniques can be found in her feature films. *Ode*'s use of subjectivity and pacing forces audiences to contemplate how they are experiencing plot information; *Then, a Year* condemns sensationalized and clichéd documentary-style form; and *Travis*, with its use of minimalism, forces viewers to experience an authentic and deeply intimate voice. Like many auteurs, Reichardt combines these cinematic characteristics, slow pacing with character intimacy and negation of mainstream expectations, and threads them into all of her subsequent features, beginning with *Old Joy*.

NOTES

1. Reichardt quoted in Ann Hornaday, "Director Kelly Reichardt on 'Meek's Cutoff' and making movies her way," *Washington Post*, 12 May 2011, <https://www.washingtonpost.com/lifestyle/style/director-kelly-reichardt-on-meeks-cutoff-and-making-movies-her-way/2011/05/08/AFOloK7G_story.html?utm_term=.74d72164158c> (accessed 20 September 2017).
2. Laura Marks, *The Skin of the Film: Intercultural Cinema, Embodiment, and the Senses* (Durham, NC: Duke University Press, 2000), p. 162.
3. Ibid. p. 163.
4. Reichardt quoted in Michael Joshua Rowin, "Q & A: Kelly Reichardt, Director of *Old Joy*," *Stop Smiling Magazine*, 22 September 2006, <http://www.stopsmilingonline.com/story_detail.php?id=655> (accessed 20 September 2017).
5. Marks, *The Skin of the Film*, p. 163.
6. Ibid. p. 162.
7. Ibid.
8. "Cold Case Files—Vanished," *ArkTV.com*, 2010.
9. Jennifer Joseph et al., "Mary Kay Letourneau Fualaau, Vili Fualaau Detail Their Path from Teacher-Student Sex Scandal to Raising Teenagers," *ABCNews.com.*, 2015, <http://abcnews.go.com/US/mary-kay-letourneau-fualaau-vili-fualaau-detail-path/story?id=30160737> (accessed 20 September 2017).
10. Ibid.
11. "James R. Hicks," *Murderpedia.org*, <http://murderpedia.org/male.H/h/hicks-james.htm> (accessed 20 September 2017).
12. Marks, *The Skin of the Film*, pp. 163–4.
13. Reichardt quoted in Rowin, "Q & A."

CHAPTER 5

Discovery: *Old Joy*

Sorrow is nothing but worn-out joy.—Kurt, *Old Joy*

*O*ld *Joy* (2006), Kelly Reichardt's second feature, stands out as her only male-centered film focusing on a male friendship and exploring alternative masculinities. Reichardt again chooses the road movie genre with a journey theme, one of self-discovery; and by avoiding content typically found in more popular "quirky" films or in "smart cinema," she focuses on social and political issues. In *Old Joy*, she introduces her audience to male stereotypes found in traditionally masculine roles and then deeply complicates them, keeping viewers off balance through intentionally ambiguous characterization. The film resists cultural constructions of masculinity and perpetuates a tradition of resistance through both questioning and offering alternative representations of social norms found in independent cinema.

Old Joy is the first of three short stories adapted by Reichardt with their author Jon Raymond. The film focuses on two men who try unsuccessfully to rekindle their past friendship. Reichardt's adaptation explores issues and types of masculinity as well as male bonding, but also creates space for a female perspective on an otherwise male-dominated narrative and genre. Throughout the film an environmental subtext is subtle but clear; Reichardt juxtaposes images of nature, civilization and technology, hinting at the damage done to natural resources while reveling in the beauty of the Oregon forest. The narrative begins with Mark (Daniel London) and Kurt (Will Oldham) setting off from Portland, Oregon for a short camping trip to Bagby Hot Springs; but once in the forest Kurt loses direction, forcing them to camp at an illegal trash dump before finding their way in the morning and arriving at the hot springs. While Reichardt depicts the effort of the two former friends' reconnection, their relationship is symbolic of a deep divide in America as it re-elected a president and continued a divisive war abroad. Reichardt addresses the environment, politics, self-discovery, and interpersonal relationships as she develops her minimalist and neorealist style. As in her other films, her aesthetics, affected by micro-budgeting, create a distinctive look, and the story is dialogue-driven and character-focused.

Raymond's short story was chosen for its minimalism and flexible budget requirements, but also because the narrative offered an artistic opportunity to film nature and explore a strained male friendship. The short story did not contain any of the political inferences, and some of the characterization was adjusted: "Mark is not married in the short story . . . He is single, so he and Kurt are closer to each other in the story; their worlds are not so far apart."[1] By adding the character of Tanya, Mark's wife, to the early scenes and then having her connect with Mark throughout the camping trip via cell phone, Reichardt adds to the depth of Mark's character, as spectators see him struggle with his multiple life roles and work to rediscover his "old free-wheeling" self and friendship with Kurt.

In an interview, Reichardt discusses Raymond's original narrative and her desire to create interpretive space for spectators:

> Jon Raymond wrote about a very personal and nuanced friendship, about the elusiveness of friendship. There's a lot of space in his writing and in my filmmaking for people to grab on to what they want and identify with what they want. I can see two people walking out of the movie and feeling completely different about it. There's space to create this kind of encounter.[2]

Reichardt intentionally leaves space throughout *Old Joy* for spectators to actively engage in their own imaginings, and when pressed in interviews about the film's messages, she encourages audiences to form their own interpretations: "I don't really want to talk about it . . . People should just watch it."[3] Her reply underscores the desire to deliver engaging and thought-provoking content without a need to assert her authorship.

PRODUCTION

Old Joy premiered at the 2006 Sundance Film Festival and was praised by critics as it traveled the festival circuit. The film was nominated for at least seven awards, winning five, with one from the Los Angeles Film Critics Association for the best independent or experimental film.[4] As with all her films, Reichardt worked diligently to stay within the independent filmmaking realm; in fact, she used a family inheritance along with other private funding to pay for *Old Joy*. In an article for *Stop Smiling* magazine, Michael Rowin explains that *Old Joy* represents the essence of true independent films: "It's not only one of the best films of the year, but perhaps the only American film of the year to superbly demonstrate the true aesthetic heritage of the term *independent*."[5] He was not the first interviewer or critic to suggest that Reichardt's process is rare; to date she has not worked with initial studio funding on any level, no matter how much easier it would make creating a film. As she explains, "The challenge with this kind of filmmaking is turning all the limitations into something that works in your favor, something that adds to the frailty of the story itself."[6] Most of *Old Joy*'s reviewers felt Reichardt was very successful in balancing her financial restraints with the possible artistic avenues of the film.

Old Joy was filmed in a minimalist style on location in natural light, with a forty-nine-page script, a six-person crew, and a two-week shooting schedule. This type of filming allows for more intimacy between actors and a deeper and more connected feeling to the natural world around them. This was important for the film, as Reichardt explains:

> as we got deeper and deeper into the forest we began shooting in a way that they [the protagonists] became more and more part of the forest. This is one of the central ideas of the film: they get lost in the forest and they become part of it and one with nature . . . by keeping the apparatus very small, it is invisible to us when we make the film. It's just six people in the woods.[7]

In *Old Joy* Reichardt uses nature as her centerpiece, with the Oregon forest almost becoming a character. While she was adapting Raymond's story, it was an art exhibit that inspired her to film in the Oregon forests after having first scouted locations in the South, "looking for swimming holes and hot springs." After those ideas led to a dead end Reichardt came back to New York and attended Justine Kurtland's photography exhibit, which helped inspire the look of the film:

> When I first got the story from Jon, I had no idea it was part of another project . . . Justine and Jon were doing a reading/slideshow . . . I was more informed by a color copy of one of the first pictures in the book, which is actually the forest around Bagby, where we ended up shooting. I had that up on my bulletin board for a long time in the search for all the other places [in the film] . . . I eventually went out to Oregon for a test shoot, out in Bagby. That photo was the real influence.[8]

Kurtland's photographs of burned forests and leafless hibernating or dead trees seem a far cry from Reichardt's shots of life-affirming streams, waterfalls, wildlife, and green forests, but the message behind both Kurtland's depictions and Reichardt's narrative aptly relate to Raymond's themes of alienation and life in a "fallen world."

While the short story held none of the political messages audiences find in the film, the politics of social and environmental issues from the short story are highlighted and mixed into the film. This is evident as Kurt and Mark's road trip begins, with scenes of Mark's Volvo driving through an industrial part of town in search of last-minute items before they head out into the Oregon wilderness. To emphasize their working-class and industrial surroundings Reichardt places her two characters in a drab industrial area, with reflections of cement mixers barreling down the road and railroad tracks embedded into paved streets. The urban setting is cross-cut with a giant concrete plant on the edge of a river, making the contrasting associations of industry and nature apparent. Beyond juxtaposing images of nature and civilization to remind viewers of social policy, she develops a subtle "nature meets technology" motif, with birds sitting on power lines, ants crawling on sidewalks, and cell phones or motor vehicles disrupting the quiet of old-growth Oregon forests. Throughout the film there is a purposeful, stark contrast created between the forest and the city, especially at the close of the film when viewers watch Kurt through a volley of passing cars and loud street noise. These scenes seem to carry a message that civilization generates chaos and distraction, while nature holds reflection and quiet.

Another element Reichardt uses to create art from nature is her decision to film in 16mm instead of the more maneuverable digital format. By using celluloid, she is able to give audiences a richer experience of the Oregon forest and stay true to her artistic visions for the film: "I really love film, and there's so much motion in this film that I don't think digital video would be the way to do it. The level of colors and depth in the forest would have not been doable in DV. I was hoping to really capture the feel of the weather, and film was necessary for this sensory element."[9] Reichardt and her director of photography Peter Sillen did not purposely resist a digital format, and even thought about other formats she had worked in extensively during her college years; but by using real film Reichardt achieved her desired aesthetic and illustrated how staying small contributes to artistic control.

Reichardt's production methods, such as using 16mm, working with independent companies, and keeping to a small crew, underscore the loyalty and dedication of her actors, her crew, and the investors who believe in her artistic vision. Filmscience founder Anish Savjani produced Reichardt's last three features, and in an interview reiterates the budget limitations on Reichardt and other indie filmmakers to adapt or create affordable scripts so their films can be produced and distributed through independent means.[10] In an interview with *Film Annex*, Savjani discusses his involvement in the film: "With *Old*

Joy, I came into the project during the post-production stage in order to raise money, and we stretched the budget . . . I usually put a half a million-dollar marker on the projects I'm going to work on. And I read the scripts with the budget in mind."[11] Savjani reiterates the budget limitations on Reichardt and other indie filmmakers to adapt or create scripts that are affordable so that their films can be produced and distributed by independent means. Kino International (now Kino Lorber) distributed *Old Joy*, and Reichardt explains how they picked up her film:

> I used to work in the mail room at Kino. I knew them . . . When we started making the film, we didn't even know if it was going to be a feature or a short so we certainly were not sure someone would pick it up. Kino was great because they are a bunch of super cinephiles, and once they showed interest it was like a dream come true. I already felt tremendously lucky making the film, so this was the icing on the cake.[12]

Finding independent avenues to produce and distribute films is "icing on the cake" because those can be daunting feats. Savjani maintains that instead of opting to release her films online, "Kelly [Reichardt] . . . is a more traditional filmmaker . . . She follows the more conventional route—theatrical, home video, and DVD. Everyone has their own distribution method . . . Kelly use[s] the press, and a lot of good press comes from the festivals."[13] It is typically at festivals that filmmakers tirelessly "shop" their films in the hope they will find distribution.

Receiving critical praise and attention is one step toward attracting a distribution company, and once that is accomplished the next step is to "use the press" through interviews, as Savjani points out, to promote the film and attract more film critic reviews. *Old Joy* challenges audiences with its pacing, content, and action (or lack thereof), so when critics suggest Reichardt's style is brave, it comes as no surprise: "About her directing, after praising her simplicity, one had to praise her daring. To make this film took considerable conviction—and, for an artist, conviction usually entails courage."[14] Reichardt's filming style is "daring," but casting male leads is a proven formula and one that sets *Old Joy* apart from her other films. Reichardt might have felt she needed two male leads, and perhaps wanted to play it safe after several years in LA promoting her project *The Royal Court*, which she felt had failed in part because it featured a black female protagonist. But if switching to male leads was a compromise, it was her only one, as *Old Joy* challenges audiences in every other way with pacing, content, and action. In one review the film was categorized as a "Listless Film" because it "carries a double melancholy for all: it makes us sad for its characters and sad for the world that has thus affected them. *Old Joy* is such a film, though it needs a bit of patience."[15]

While some critics might use "patience" as a warning to viewers that the film is slow-paced in terms of action even though it falls into the "road movie/buddy" genre, Reichardt prefers the word "deliberate" as a better descriptor for the camera shots: "It's static, but it's not always static. It's not Jarmusch. In addition, there are many things crossing through the frame. The camera is deliberate."[16] Reichardt credits the films of Yasujirō Ozu and Satyajit Ray as influencing her "static" framing of landscapes throughout *Old Joy*:[17] "Last year in New York we had a full month of Ozu films. He also has a very steady camera and amazingly interesting framings."[18] Her choice to present framed wildlife or landscape clearly shows Ozu's influence. Another probable model was "Satyajit Ray's films and the ways he deals with nature . . . If I had to say which one of these is my main influence I'd say Ray."[19] Through her use of static shots and deliberate filming, Reichardt creates deeper and more complex characterizations by employing slow cinematic techniques such as real-time pacing, long silences or pauses, and relying on dialogue versus action to progress the plot.

COMPLICATING MASCULINITY

In many ways this slow aesthetic allows Reichardt to complicate her depictions of masculinity, so that viewers struggle to label Kurt and Mark's relationship. Kurt is described as "a post-hippie with never-present promise," while Mark has a more flattering introduction as "the father-to-be, intent on putting the Kurt part of his life behind him."[20] The desire to label them with neat, easily understood gender identities is tempting, but Reichardt's nuances keep audiences guessing. What makes Kurt so much more complicated is not only his sexual ambiguity and liberal philosophies, but Reichardt's use of realism and minimalism in his depiction: she has scripted a realistic personality whose flaws have a distancing effect on the spectator. One critic wrote: "Will Oldham plays Kurt like a man who has survived an existence that was supposed to have nullified him and who has some quiet pride in it."[21]

Reichardt counts on the fact that American viewers, who are so driven to "grow up" and "make something of themselves," will be both jealous of Kurt and appalled by him. While jealousy might not seem an appropriate reaction, Reichardt considers the idea that Mark is jealous of Kurt's life, so by extension her audience might be as well: "Is Mark jealous that Kurt is free? This is a possibility the film opens up. Ultimately . . . I have gone out of the way in the filmmaking to leave these possibilities open . . . there are so many ways to read each of the characters."[22] Kurt is the persona many overworked and exhausted Americans secretly wish they could assume. Reichardt exposes this stereotype, and in an interview she explains the perceptions around the character: "You're living a certain way in your twenties that may be romantic, but when you get to your mid-thirties and you have that same lifestyle it becomes slightly question-able and taxing to people's lives that you move in and out of . . . My freedom at the expense of everyone I know, basically."[23] In the same interview, Reichardt discusses how she and Will Oldham worked to cast a "real" Kurt in the role, but were unsuccessful: "Will ended up in the Kurt role. For a while he was trying to turn me on to people he knew who were 'truly Kurt.' People living in their van, no phone, and two months later they'd call—'Hey, I'm a friend of Will's.' Okay, that won't work for a movie."[24] Spectators are jealous that Kurt has survived that "nullified" existence, but they also see the downfalls of such a lifestyle.

If Kurt has any power at all in society, it is a "fleeting nostalgia for missed freedom." [25] In his work "Masculinity as Homophobia," Michael Kimmel touches on masculine power in American society, explaining that "[m]anhood is equated with power—over women, over other men."[26] Mark is struggling with rekindling his friendship with Kurt because Kurt represents men who are powerless as deemed by society—and according to Kimmel, if Mark recon-nects fully with Kurt, he too will be relinquishing his access to power. Kimmel speaks to Mark's reluctance:

> In contrast to women's lives, men's lives are structured around relation-ships of power and men's differential access to power, as well as the dif-ferential access to that power of men as a group. Our imperfect analysis of our own situation leads us to believe that we men need more power, rather than leading us to support feminists' efforts to rearrange power relationships along more equitable lines.[27]

Mark has worked hard to attain a certain status in society, and whether or not he is happy, he has managed to achieve and affirm his access to power through normative masculinity since his days with Kurt. Michael Kimmel discusses further why men feel so powerless that they constantly strive to align them-selves with a hegemonic masculine ideology: "the rules of manhood [imply] that only the tiniest fraction of men come to believe that they are the biggest of wheels, the sturdiest of oaks, the most virulent repudiators of femininity . . . We've managed to disempower the overwhelming majority of American men by other means—such as discriminat[ion]." [28] There is no attempt to fit Kurt into the cultural normalization that Mark has experienced through keeping a job, marrying, and preparing to raise a child. In fact, audiences work to iden-tify with Mark, who according to society's rules has his "life together" and his "priorities straight," but as the film progresses Reichardt cleverly creates a tug of war with viewers' emotional allegiance as they bounce from one character to the other, finding points of identification as well as frustration.

Figure 5.1 Mark and Kurt on the sidewalk

Kurt does not just represent a "free spirit," as described by Daniel London in an interview;[29] from the beginning, his actions spell out someone who is unreliable, opportunistic, confused, and lazy. After Mark has worked out his trip with Tanya he arrives to an empty house, and after knocking and tapping on doors and windows he sits for an unspecified amount of time on the front porch waiting for Kurt to arrive. Viewers feel relief when Kurt shows up, since they are invested in Mark, having watched his struggles, and form a reserved opinion of Kurt as his fuzzy form appears across the street, pulling a child's Radio wagon with a TV precariously perched inside and holding a borrowed green cooler (Figure 5.1). He is late, his wrinkled shirt is unevenly buttoned, and he shows no remorse for making Mark wait and wonder about his whereabouts. This scene foreshadows the "lost" scenes later in the film in which Kurt, after assuring Mark he knows where they are, keeps them driving in the Oregon woods until well past nightfall, never finding the original campsite, so that they end up having to camp near an illegal trash dump. But even with the many signals audiences receive about Kurt's unsympathetic characterization, his honesty and vulnerability concerning his desire for a renewed friendship—the very qualities that make him powerless in a hyper-masculine society—keep viewers invested.

To the frustration of spectators, Reichardt deliberately leaves the men's previous relationship undefined, making viewers work to understand and process their friendship. The underlying tension between Kurt and Mark might not be about whether or not they were lovers, but rather whether Mark will open up to Kurt and show any emotional vulnerability. Audiences keep waiting, but

Mark simply cannot allow himself to reclaim their earlier friendship in all its manifestations. This friendship was once a safe space for both of them, and not the debilitating cycle Kimmel describes in his chapter: "As young men we are constantly riding those gender boundaries, checking the fences we have constructed on the perimeter, making sure that nothing even remotely feminine might show through. The possibilities of being unmasked are everywhere."[30] Kurt and Mark were able to find a comfortable and intimate male friendship in their past, and while we see their struggle to find that place again throughout the film, the struggle reaches an emotional climax during the campfire scene. As Kurt begins the pivotal conversation in which he attempts to explain his interpretation of string theory, the metaphors are thick: "The entire universe is in the shape of a tear falling down through space. This tear has been dropping now forever; it just doesn't stop." Spectators quickly realize that Kurt is talking about his emotional perception of the world, and specifically his feelings about the lost friendship he has not been able to rekindle during the trip with Mark (Figure 5.2). Kurt continues by saying, "I miss you, Mark. I miss you really really bad. I want us to be real friends again. There is something between us and I don't like it. I want it to go away." This type of open and honest confession leaves Kurt vulnerable, but his depth is not matched by Mark, who instead works to pacify and deny any issues by saying, "We're fine. We're totally fine." Kurt has no recourse but to apologize for his emotional plea and retreat: "God, I'm sorry. I'm just being crazy. I'm sorry. I'm just being crazy. I know. Don't pay any attention to me. We're fine. Everything is totally fine. I feel a lot better now." This is Mark's chance to talk to Kurt about the real issue between them, but Mark cannot bring himself to do it. Clearly

Figure 5.2 Mark and Kurt camping at a trash dump

Kurt desires the ability to be with another man beyond what Kimmel calls "riding those gender boundaries."

Reichardt is testing audience expectations by placing such an emotional and intimate scene at night, right before the two characters share a tent. Spectators wonder if they were sexually intimate in the past, and whether the relationship will reignite that evening. Critics discussed how the film frustrates boundaries "between camaraderie, male bonding, and homoeroticism with the possible homosexuality of Kurt and Mark."[31] Could it be, however, that audiences conditioned by mainstream expectations do not know what to make of male friendship in the absence of adventure, violence, women, comedy, and children? After all, there are no superpowers or extraordinary distractions for the duo to handle, no urgency to save the day or take revenge. Offering a visual metaphor for the path of their friendship the following morning, the camera cuts between a beautiful cloudy sky and shots of decaying trash, with the dump that they were forced to camp at reflecting the gradual decay of their friendship.

In addition to ambiguous male relationships, Reichardt toys with the road movie genre by leaving out a central theme: violent acts. Kimmel elaborates on how violence functions in society, saying, "Violence is often the single most evident marker of manhood. Rather it is the willingness to fight, the desire to fight," and Reichardt, as she portrays men working on a friendship, opts to leave violence out of *Old Joy*.[32] Reichardt took a risk by not including action or violence. While the lack of action keeps a production budget manageable, a study by Cerridwen and Simonton shows that when American audiences go to movies, violence and suspense appear to be a draw: "violence tends to have a positive effect on U.S. and world gross, a pattern paralleled by guns/weapons."[33] In *Old Joy*, instead of violence, spectators see laughter, nostalgia, intimacy, frustration, angst, deep sadness, and a sense of loss or regret. There is no fight scene, no blood, no death or abusive shouting; and the lack of traditional masculinity cues for the American spectator translates into ambiguity, which creates active and engaged discovery. Cerridwen and Simonton also found films that had "a larger proportion of women as producers, directors, writers or actors . . . displayed much less violence, including less weaponry, fear-inducing editing and music, blood and gore, and so forth. At the same time, the female presence shows up in more thought-provoking films."[34] Instead of explicit violence, Reichardt creates suspense by denying spectators easily defined gender roles through traditional cues. She gives audiences a long overdue opportunity, no matter how exhausting or uncomfortable, to confront an alternative masculinity, culminating in the sequence when Kurt and Mark reach their bathhouse destination.

The bathhouse represents more than just a hot springs. It is portrayed as a safe space for homosocial intimacies and connection. Even though the bathhouse was in high demand at the time of the shoot, it is depicted as a place where nature offers soothing calm and peaceful rejuvenation for hikers. Part of what makes the bathhouse safe is the shared rituals and traditions of the activity. Each step of the characters' progress toward experiencing the baths is recorded, from their excitement at arriving to relaxing in the tubs and telling stories. It is clear that Kurt holds the power in these scenes. He is in charge of the action, and he maintains that authority through language: he gives detailed instructions to Mark on how to plug up the tubs and use the buckets, and he is even comfortable enough to toss Mark a beer. One reason for this might be that Kurt is making up for delaying them with his navigational failure the previous night; but either way, these hiking and camping rituals reinforce their male camaraderie, which facilitates working toward a common goal. Kurt's storytelling is another sign of his authority, but it also shows his openness and desire for reconciliation. His newfound authority might also explain why he feels empowered to rub Mark's shoulders at the conclusion of his story, which holds the title of the film: "Sorrow is nothing but worn-out joy."

When Kurt stands up after concluding his story, he approaches the tub in which Mark is soaking, eyes closed, and begins to rub his shoulders. Mark's initial reaction is one of surprise, saying, "Hey, what's going on?" and Kurt quickly asserts his control over the situation, replying, "Just relax, man; just settle in." Viewers cannot tell if Mark is merely tolerating Kurt, or if he is really giving himself over to the moment, since actor Daniel London keeps Mark's character emotionally inaccessible. Reichardt's use of suggestive and sensual imagery to indicate her characters' internal communications and connections leaves little doubt that they have shared a moment (Figure 5.3). While the moment is ambiguous, sensual images such as Mark's wedding-banded

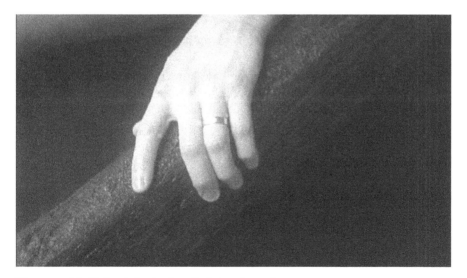

Figure 5.3 Mark's hand slipping into the hot springs tub

hand slowly releasing its grip on his tub and falling into the water, followed by cascading water drops, running water down a long wooden gutter, bubbling waterfalls, and steam drifting out of the bathhouse, all indicate a deep connection between the two friends. While the bathhouse scene is homoerotic, indicated by the release of tension in Mark and the sexualized images of nature afterwards, it also illustrates Kurt's empowerment and implied responsibility for Mark's "back to nature" experience. During the film festival circuit tour, critics debated as to the nature of their relationship, referring to imagery in the bathhouse scene such as their feet sticking out of the tubs as if they were tangled together after sex, a slug on a flower, and Mark's looks of ecstasy. Some reviews, however, such as one by critic Manohlia Dargis, conclude that there was no romantic intention in Reichardt's characterization: "Much like Ms. Reichardt's first feature, *River of Grass* (1995), about a young woman who dreams of escaping her dreary life by going on the lam, *Old Joy* briefly borrows the conventions of the road movie while keeping its romance safely at bay."[35] In his article "Dude, Where's My Gender," David Green notes that while there may be safe spaces in public for male "homosocial" interaction (such as the bathhouse), our society does not expect those spaces to be used in a sexualized manner: "The term 'homosocial' . . . succinctly describes the sphere and realms of same-sex relations—the relationships and spaces in which both male power and intimacy are concentrated. Homosocial relations may include homosexual ones, but, in our homophobic culture, they are not meant to."[36] While critics and audiences will have to be satisfied with the ambiguity of their relationship, it is clear that Reichardt wants to discuss more than masculinity and sexuality through her characters.

POLITICS AND PERSONAL IDENTITY

As with all of her films, Reichardt insinuates a political failing, and this time it is by the George W. Bush administration. The deep divide between Mark and Kurt is mirrored in several driving scenes in which Mark listens to Air America radio as divisions between political parties and stances are hashed out. Air America talk radio is heard from the moment the two begin their trip until they reach a bridge leading out of town. It serves almost as a physical barrier for the protagonists and for spectators, as Air America is not heard again until Mark drops Kurt off at the end of the film. Throughout the montage of scenes, even though there is some dialogue and a hint of background music, Air America's commentary is front and center, reminding audiences of the frustration and impotence of liberals and the Democratic Party in the early 2000s. In an interview, Reichardt talks about her intentions: "I did want to set the exact period of time when Bush was re-elected, not just a loss, but another old joy: both elections were stolen, the loss of democracy . . . the Air America segments—that's just liberals fighting amongst themselves."[37] As evidence, there is a radio clip of commentary about how the presidential candidate missed an opportunity to champion the working class and go after corporate corruption. This conversation is perfectly matched by the industrial backdrop and creates a subtle political commentary. Reichardt sheds light on how including these radio segments underscores the politics behind the film: "As a viewer you experience these crazy, arguing voices, and by the tone of it you encounter politics . . . During the John Kerry campaign you could see the Democrats were really lost. To sum it up: liberalism has become a dirty word . . . these are two friends who embark on a weekend trip to connect, and they can't . . . There is a feeling that the Democratic party has struggled to do this as well."[38]

Reichardt's insertion of politics through the use of radio segments captures America's deep political division in that time period characterized by Manohla Dargis: "progressive radio . . . delivers the relentless grind of bad news that Mark can only listen to without comment and with a face locked in worry, a face on which Ms. Reichardt invites us to project the shell shock, despair and hopelessness of everyone else listening in across the country."[39] Dargis refers to the displacement liberals in America felt during the 2001–9 presidency of George W. Bush, when many of their social and political ideas, ranging from a mishandled election to greenhouse gas emissions, were blocked or vetoed. Vicente Rodriguez-Ortega agrees with Dargis's assessment, adding "[t]he result [*Old Joy*] is beautifully minimalist, capturing in visual terms the disenchantment of the Left in the current era of rampant conservatism."[40] Though Mark is an example of a liberal who does nothing but "worry" and listen to divisive talk radio, Reichardt signals that action is needed: "Mark is not really doing anything . . . as if the act of listening is enough. At the end of the day Mark is this guy that wants world peace. However, he needs to connect with a friend or his wife about this, but he is unable to cross the bridge so it makes one feel defeated about the bigger picture."[41] She mentions her own need to make a statement about where America was during this time period:

I know I'm not capable of making an out-and out political film, but I did think there were elements in the film of what I was experiencing—ineffectualness . . . I concentrated on the friendship—the other stuff [political comments] were ideas for myself, ideas that make you feel like you're doing something relevant.[42]

Reichardt fulfills her wish to be "relevant" by inserting political commentary into what might seem to be an apolitical narrative, hinting at multiple connections between the personal and the political, masculinity and power.

While Kurt and Mark's friendship can be symbolic of the ineffectual political parties in America, the desire to reconnect to a past friend and, in doing so, reassert a personal identity is a universal theme. Interestingly enough, Reichardt depicts this reasserting with very sparse dialogue. From the first moment Kurt and Mark see each other, their relationship is defined by the use of silence. After they greet each other at the beginning of the film and stand beside Kurt's van, Mark asks Kurt: "How was Ashland?" From the moment he asks the question, Mark stares directly into Kurt's face, unwaveringly, with narrowed eyes, as if to pry the truth out. Mark is searching to see if he would have had the same experience as Kurt if he had been at the retreat. The silence between Mark's question and the broken reply from Kurt speaks volumes. "Ashland" represents a trip Mark could not participate in because of his social and domestic responsibilities and expectations, and he is frustrated by Kurt's ability to live in seeming freedom.

Kurt replies, "Ashland?!" with a question in his voice, as if he has to remember, signifying that he has experienced many "Ashlands," unlike Mark. Kurt pauses, making Mark wait, and then says, "Amazing [pause] transformative [pause] I'm at a whole new place now [pause] really," his long pauses betraying a need to convince himself that he really is at this "new place." The power dynamic that happens within the silences speaks to Kimmel's suggestion that men feel masculinity is about who appears the "biggest of wheels." Kurt is struggling to hold on to his "free spirit" identity as a traveling Renaissance man, while fighting the inevitable judgment he knows will come from Mark. At this point in his life, it is likely that Kurt deals with judgments about his lifestyle and identity from a number of friends who have normed themselves with a hegemonic masculinity.

The silence after Kurt proclaims his experience in Ashland was "transformative," along with Mark's steady, piercing gaze, freeze Kurt for a moment, until the tension becomes uncomfortable and Kurt gives way by shaking his head "no" and shifting his eyes downward. Mark's next remark refers to all the clutter collected in Kurt's van as they look into the opened back door, but it resonates with the silence they have just shared: "Wow—you really have it all goin' on." Kurt replies, "Hell yeah—where's your shit?" Mark means that Kurt seems to have his life figured out, and is still living in twentysomething "freedomland," especially after his intentionally ambiguous statement about being transformed by the recent retreat. But there is a laugh in Mark's voice, showing that he does not believe Kurt; Mark is struggling to take the power back from Kurt, and Kurt's reply to this is "Where's your shit?" Of course he means camping gear, but metaphorically Mark's "shit" is at home, in the form of a mortgage, a job, and pregnant partner. His material existence is too involved to fit into the back of a van. This is yet another indication that Mark's chosen normative path in society weighs heavily.

INSERTING THE FEMININE

Although *Old Joy* seems to be primarily about masculinity and relationships between men, it is also concerned with male-female relationships, the uncertainties of pregnancy, and Mark's looming family responsibilities. At the opening of the film spectators are greeted by birds chirping, the sound of humming Tibetan bowls, and images of animals in nature. Audiences move from nature sounds mixed with the chimes of meditation aids while Mark sits cross-legged, barefoot, in his grassy yard, to an abrupt cut of Tanya, his very pregnant wife, loudly blending a smoothie, listening to the radio, and a phone ringing. Reichardt uses sound and images to illustrate the intrusiveness of technology, and references gender stereotypes by drawing boundaries between the domestic inside world of the home that Tanya occupies and the outside world of nature that Mark and Kurt inhabit. As Mark struggles to meditate outside with the sound of children playing, Tanya seems to stay in a mindless meditation inside even though she is surrounded by noise and interruptions. The dull look in her eyes changes only slightly as she hears Kurt leave a message for Mark about camping that evening. Viewers are denied a close-up of her face as she taps her fingers on the doorway and stares down at the machine.

Reichardt is saying volumes with Tanya in a very short period of time, considering she is only on screen for three to four minutes. The first, and shallower, interpretation might unfortunately be the most popular: Tanya is self-absorbed and miserable, and therefore wants her partner to suffer as well. There should be no changes, fun, or newness in either of their lives. But this reading and quick judgment of Tanya are complicated by Reichardt's depiction. Tanya seems ready to be done with pregnancy and to own her body again; this might explain why her gaze is inward, even with all the distractions present in her first scenes. She is also aware that any time Kurt visits, she loses her partner for a period of time. Reichardt creates several cues that contribute to a very fair picture of Tanya, allowing audiences to understand their relationship. After all, Tanya does not have to tell Mark about the message; she could delete it, knowing Kurt will probably move on to another friend. Reichardt agrees that Kurt might have found another camping buddy: "I don't necessarily think that Mark was the first person that Kurt called that day."[43] And she backs this assertion up in the script, when later, upon the men's first face-to-face meeting in the film, Kurt says, "I'm really glad you could come. I didn't know if you could make it on such short notice—everyone is so busy now." Kurt basically confesses that Mark was not the first, nor would he have been the last call Kurt made to invite a friend to camp. As the machine clicks off, the camera cuts to more power lines and birds outside, and spectators hear Mark greeting Kurt on the phone. Tanya until this point has been pretending to be uninterested, with her back to the couple on the phone, until actual plans begin to form and Mark sounds as if he is committing; then she inserts her body physically into their conversation as a reminder to Mark that he has responsibilities. Their lack of sustained eye contact indicates that each wants something they are not getting from the other: Tanya wants Mark to reject the trip on his own, noting that he is now a "family man" and understands he is needed at home, while Mark wants his partner to give him permission to be free and return, briefly, to what he sees himself giving up for marriage and family. Reichardt inserts a theme common to many relationships through Tanya's dialogue: "Look, we're just waiting for me to tell you, you can go. We know you're going, so I don't know why we have to go through this thing of me letting you off the hook." While the close-up shots of each are almost equal in number, they tend to linger on Tanya, and audiences might see this as a suggestion of who they should side with; however, Reichardt complicates the interactions by playing off the stereotype of a "nagging" wife who will not allow her husband any freedom. Visually the shots support Tanya's reasoning, but emotionally spectators are probably quick to come to Mark's aid. Reichardt is working to hold a mirror up to her audience, and through the use of close-ups she leaves spectators squirming in their seats as they witness the emotional exchange.

In this sequence Reichardt achieves a realistic exchange with her use of minimalism suggesting universal themes of marital conflict. The last shot of the exchange is of Tanya's face, with downcast eyes but with traces of defiance which, the audience can guess, will fade to hopeless resolution. The sound of a lawnmower begins before we cut to Mark packing up the car and loading his dog, Wendy, into his Volvo station wagon. The camera lingers on the closed trunk, while in an unfocused background a woman mows her yard. Reichardt seems to be saying that while Mark goes off to play, women stay home and take care of the chores, whether inside or outside. The last we see of Tanya is a side profile shot from behind in a very quiet house as she looks down and then back up again. In that moment, audiences take in the full extent of her unhappiness. For a film with two male protagonists, Reichardt outlines so much about pregnancy and motherhood: the frustrations, worry, boredom, and uncertainty. Spectators wonder if Mark is truly ready for fatherhood, and that sets up Mark's quest narrative as he goes in search of what he has lost—freedom and male bonds—but ends up reaffirming the embrace of socially dictated behavior and responsibility codes. Only during the climax of the film, in the bathhouse, does Mark seem to accomplish his goal and completely lose himself to a fleeting moment of freedom.

Reichardt concludes Mark's story as he drives home looking reflective—but not about his camping experience—while we hear Air America once again discussing political stagnation. The announcer mirrors Mark's anxiety about becoming a father and taking on socially acceptable roles when he refers to the cost of ignoring labor and environmental issues: "When you notice that housing costs, health care costs, and energy costs are exploding, you're talking about things that make up the overwhelming share of the budget of an ordinary family. And so the combination of the uncertainty of the future and the pressure on the present create this move." Air America bookends the film, reminding viewers of Mark's political nature while reinforcing the parallel between his and Kurt's irreconcilable friendship and America's divided political landscape. The words "uncertainty" and "pressure" used in the segment also echo Mark's fears of becoming a father. Kurt's future, however, is much more uncertain than Mark's, as Reichardt's cinematic choices illustrate (Figure 5.4). Filming from across a busy street, the camera zooms in to capture Kurt wandering aimlessly, as if in a daze, unable to decide his direction. The use of selective focus with a zoom creates distance and underscores the audience's voyeuristic connection to Kurt versus the earlier, more intimate audience relationship. Reichardt wants to remind viewers that Kurt is socially undesirable. By creating a connection to an "other" and then displacing that connection, Reichardt is reiterating the damage done to individuals when they are stereotyped and the importance of underfunded social entities such as homeless shelters. Audiences are not allowed to follow Kurt, as his path is too sporadic and "uncertain." *Old Joy*'s sad and open ending leaves viewers wondering if Kurt and Mark will ever see each other again, and if Kurt will survive his wanderlust. Much like in *Wendy and Lucy*, Reichardt's third feature, audiences see their protagonists adrift in a society that demands conformity while offering little to no hope of a sustainable future.

Figure 5.4 Kurt wandering aimlessly

NOTES

E. Dawn Hall, "*Old Joy* (2006): Resisting Masculinity," in Claire Perkins and Constantine Verevis (eds.), *US Independent Film After 1989: Possible Films* (Edinburgh: Edinburgh University Press, 2015), pp. 123–32.

1. Reichardt quoted in Vicente Rodriguez-Ortega, "New Voice: An Interview with Kelly Reichardt," *Reverse Shot*, 18 September 2006, <http://reverseshot.org/interviews/entry/804/kelly-reichardt> (accessed 20 September 2017).
2. Ibid.
3. Ibid.
4. "*Old Joy* (2006): Awards," *Internet Movie Database*, <http://www.imdb.com/title/tt0468526/awards?ref_=tt_awd> (accessed 20 September 2017).
5. Michael Joshua Rowin, "Q & A: Kelly Reichardt, Director of *Old Joy*," *Stop Smiling Magazine*, 22 September 2006, <http://www.stopsmilingonline.com/story_detail.php?id=655> (accessed 20 September 2017).
6. Kelly Reichardt, "*Old Joy* Director's Statement," Museum of the Moving Image Series *Adrift in America: The Films of Kelly Reichardt*, 3 April 2011.
7. Reichardt quoted in Rowin, "Q & A."
8. Ibid.
9. Reichardt quoted in Rodriguez-Ortega, "New Voice."
10. Anish Savjani quoted in Eren Gulfidan, "Interview with Anish Savjani, the producer of *Wendy and Lucy*," *Film Annex*, 19 January 2008.
11. Ibid.
12. Reichardt quoted in Rodriguez-Ortega, "New Voice."
13. Savjani quoted in Gulfidan, "Interview."
14. Stanley Kauffmann, "Parting of Ways," *The New Republic* (October 2006), p. 29.
15. Ibid. p. 28.
16. Reichardt quoted in Rodriguez-Ortega, "New Voice."
17. Ibid.
18. Ibid.
19. Ibid.
20. *Old Joy* DVD cover (KINO International, 2004).
21. Kauffmann, "Parting," p. 29.
22. Reichardt quoted in Rodriguez-Ortega, "New Voice."
23. Reichardt quoted in Rowin, "Q & A."
24. Ibid.
25. Michael Kimmel, "Masculinity as Homophobia," in Estelle Disch (ed.), *Reconstructing Gender: A Multicultural Anthology* (Boston: McGraw Hill, 2004), p. 106.
26. Ibid.
27. Ibid. p. 107.
28. Ibid. p. 108.
29. "Old Joy—Daniel London and Kelly Reichardt Interview," YouTube video posted by BBC Collective, 8 August 2007, <https://www.youtube.com/watch?v=RKJgxh3PQDM> (accessed 20 September 2017).
30. Michael Kimmel, *The History of Men* (New York: State University of New York Press, 2005), p. 184.
31. John Esther, "GLBT Films Keep Comin' At Sundance '06," *Gay & Lesbian Review Worldwide* 13, no. 3 (2006).

32. Kimmel, "Masculinity as Homophobia," p. 104.
33. Cerridwen, Anemone and Dean K. Simonton, "Sex Doesn't Sell—Nor Impress! Content, Box Office, Critics, and Awards in Mainstream Cinema," *Psychology of Aesthetics, Creativity and the Arts* 3, no. 4 (2009): 204, <https://www.apa.org/pubs/journals/releases/aca-3-4-200.pdf> (accessed 17 September 2017).
34. Ibid. p. 208.
35. Manohla Dargis, "A Journey Through Forests and a Sense of Regret," *The New York Times*, 20 September 2006, <http://www.nytimes.com/2006/09/20/movies/a-journey-through-forests-and-a-sense-of-regret.html> (accessed 20 September 2017).
36. David Green, "Dude, Where's My Gender? Contemporary Teen Comedies and New Forms of American Masculinity," *Cineaste* (July 2002), p. 15.
37. Reichardt quoted in Rowin, "Q & A."
38. Reichardt quoted in Rodriguez-Ortega, "New Voice."
39. Dargis, "A Journey Through Forests."
40. Rodriguez-Ortega, "New Voice."
41. Reichardt quoted in Rodriguez-Ortega, "New Voice."
42. Reichardt quoted in Rowin, "Q & A."
43. Ibid.

CHAPTER 6

Breakthrough: *Wendy and Lucy*

You can't get an address without an address. You can't get a job without a job. It's all fixed. —Wally, *Wendy and Lucy*

*W*endy and Lucy* (2008), Reichardt's third feature, builds on the mixed-genre tradition of her earlier films; the film draws on the road movie genre, but denies the full experience in an effort to convey social and political messages. While the narrative unravels in a small Oregon town within the span of a few days, Reichardt uses it to broaden viewers' perspectives and assumptions about the identities and lives of lower-working-class and homeless Americans. By casting a young woman as her protagonist, she complicates issues of homelessness and poverty through the lens of gender. She contributes to conversations surrounding girlhood, specifically Anita Harris's social commentary surrounding the commodification of girlhood in a consumer culture. By connecting ecofeminism to Reichardt's content, the film explores a capitalist culture's effects on marginalized members of the population.

Wendy and Lucy follows Wendy Carroll (Michelle Williams) as she journeys across America to find work in the Alaskan canneries. When her car breaks down and her dog Lucy is lost, she meets Wally (Walter Dalton), a sympathetic Walgreen's security guard whose situation gives voice to the working-class poor. He provides a cell phone number for her lost dog posters and hands her what he can afford to spare—six dollars—as a going-away present. In an effort to repair her only means of shelter and transportation Wendy engages with an unsympathetic mechanic, Bill (Will Patton), whose reactions represent capitalist ideology; his news that her car is unfixable leaves Wendy homeless. Much as Reichardt manages the challenges of her micro-budget filmmaking, Wendy wrestles to control her future by being creative, determined, and owning her choices, no matter how difficult. In the same spirit, Reichardt's definition of success rests outside the mainstream standards.

PRODUCTION

Wendy and Lucy premiered at the 46th Annual New York Film Festival's Forum in September 2008 before making its rounds to multiple film festivals such as the Toronto International, Chicago International, and Cannes. In competition, the film won AFI's Movie of the Year award and NBR's award for Top Independent Film, and was nominated for six others.[1] *Wendy and Lucy* made approximately $1,192,655 worldwide and had a domestic total gross of $865,695.[2] It was important to Reichardt that these totals be moderately profitable for the production and distribution companies. As she explains, keeping a solid filmmaking team is important to her artistic process: "I'm trying to surround myself with people that know me and give me the space to do that [be creative] and that's been very hard to find."[3] Both production companies on *Wendy and Lucy* were repeat collaborators for Reichardt: Glass Eye Pix helped to produce *River of Grass* and Filmscience, along with others, produced *Old Joy*. In addition Reichardt hired independent producer Neil Kopp, a staple in her team ever since, explaining that "Neil can get his head around how he can physically make it [the film] happen while keeping the budget as low as possible. I do try and set up the production in a way that it creates an atmosphere that I can be creative in."[4] Another familiar face in Reichardt's team was Jon Raymond, whose short story "Train Choir" was the basis for the film. Reichardt thought the original title was too "poetic," so she opted for *Wendy and Lucy*, which features the co-star, her own dog Lucy.[5] Raymond and Reichardt worked together to adapt his story into a screenplay, just as they had done with *Old Joy*: "With *Wendy and Lucy*, we devised the storyline together, and then he went off to write it as a full-fledged short story. Jon's interested in writing about landscapes, narratives of the road, friendships—themes that are close to my own interests."[6] The only newcomer was Oscilloscope Laboratories, a New York-based company established in 2008 by Adam Yauch (formerly of the music group Beastie Boys), which distributed the film and stayed on to distribute her next feature, *Meek's Cutoff* (2010). When Oscilloscope's co-founder David Fenkel, formerly of FilmThink, was asked how his company selected *Wendy and Lucy*, which "helped seal Oscilloscope's reputation for quality and good results," he explained:

> The film had a marquee name and great buzz. And we were all very passionate about it. It did under a million theatrically but was very cost-effective. The budget to make the film was frugal and the release wasn't

advertising-driven, which drives up costs . . . There was also much critical support. We also carefully positioned it as a prestigious film by setting
the release date for December. And we did very well in ancillary because
the theatrical release caught the attention of big-box retailers like Best
Buy who took us on.[7]

Budget concerns are never far from independent filmmakers' minds, and
Reichardt's budget has grown slightly with each feature film. At its release, the
$300,000 budget for *Wendy and Lucy* was her largest yet. From the opening
scenes, however, her ability to stretch a small budget speaks to her typical
aesthetic, a minimalist neorealistic style. During the opening scenes Reichardt
uses natural lighting and source sound as Wendy and her dog Lucy walk beside
a train track. She takes advantage of the established train track to create a
long dolly shot. As Lucy is Reichardt's own pet there is no need for an animal
handler, and the only soundtrack for the moment is Wendy's humming. Wendy
searches for Lucy, and as dusk falls she finds her dog with a group of "gutter
punks" sitting around a fire. Much like Eisenstein's *lumpenproletariat*, who
represent the immediate environment coming alive in *Strike* (1925), the train-
hopping group symbolizes Wendy's future: socially deemed throwaways. The
exposition scenes after the film's title credits are shot using that large campfire,
which serves to create shadows across Wendy's anxious face and reinforces the
instability and vulnerability of her existence. Reichardt uses non-actors, except
for Icky (Will Oldham), for the group of travelers camping by the tracks that
evening. She discusses the challenges and opportunities in working with those
non-actors in a *Bomb* interview with Gus Van Sant, explaining that while they
did fit the micro-budget film's needs, they came with strings attached:

> They *are* authentic train-hopping gutter punks. That was one of the
> hardest nights of shooting. They were demanding drugs and alcohol, and
> some of them were really young and pissed that we weren't getting them
> drunk. A lot is gained by them being authentic, I loved shooting them
> through the firelight; I mean, their faces are amazing.[8]

And while Reichardt cleverly uses any available resource to shoot her films as
a matter of necessity, experiences of that type cultivate her appreciation for
trained actors:

> I've become completely sold on the art of acting over the years. It's great
> to be able to do nuanced things with an actor like Michelle who is really
> a master of her craft. I always thought it would be easier shooting with
> non-actors. If you love what they're doing when they're doing it, then
> it's the greatest, but if you want to change anything, it is very difficult.[9]

Reichardt explained that by disguising Williams, they were able to enjoy some anonymity while filming: "Michelle really loved the way she was so invisible as Wendy, how she slipped into this landscape; I don't remember anybody recognizing her during shooting. We didn't have the manpower to close off streets, and so it was important to slip into the environment relatively unnoticed."[10] During another outdoor scene Wendy encounters a violent homeless man played by Larry Fessenden (co-founder of Glass Eye Pix, a co-producer of the film and the male lead in *River of Grass* [1995]). Cutting costs by limiting personnel to six named actors and ten to thirteen crew members, casting production members as actors, and utilizing non-actors, Reichardt demonstrates the ingenuity necessary for micro-budget indie filmmaking.

While practical decisions about production are driven in part by budget concerns, they are also influenced by the aesthetic Reichardt strives to convey. Because she adheres to a minimalist style, Reichardt is very deliberate about her decisions with sound throughout the film. The only soundtrack other than source sound is the "Wendy Theme Music." Spectators are introduced to this whimsical hum during the opening shot of Wendy walking and playing with Lucy, and immediately begin to associate Wendy with the song. Williams was asked about the creation of the "Wendy Theme Music" during a question and answer session at the film's premier:

> I spend a lot of time preparing for it [the role] alone . . . There is something you do when you are unobserved for hours and hours and hours on end [as the role required]. I thought about humming and every time I would hum I would find myself humming a copyright song. I couldn't make my own melody . . . [Will Oldham] threw me a song with guitar picking . . . so it is some combination of his song and something in my head.[11]

A variation on Williams's humming can be heard broadcast over the grocery store sound system when Wendy enters to steal dog food. It is another way to imprint her theme music on the audience and was arranged by Smokey Hormel, a musician who worked with Reichardt on *Old Joy*. Apart from the "Wendy Theme Music," Reichardt opted for naturally occurring sound. Barking dogs in an animal shelter, busy traffic at a four-way intersection, doves cooing on electrical lines, starts and stops from a bus, Mattress World advertisements and even Wendy's tears and sobs are all used as a soundtrack throughout the film. Besides the hum, the most iconic sounds Reichardt inserts are of the trains. She explains her process by saying: "I do have a list of sounds that I want when we start filming . . . I just didn't want to romanticize the film in any way. I tried to use the train and traffic as I would use a score."[12] The film opens in a train yard and closes in one, with train tracks featured throughout, so viewers have a foreshadowing of the last scene. While it might seem like a simple matter of recording actual trains, filming logistics are a challenge: "Recording trains is just so incredibly hard. They're far, and then they're close, and when they're close, they're noisy. So some of these trains are stolen from Gus Van Sant's *Paranoid Park*, trains they didn't use . . . I was like, 'I need a train! Yours are so much better than ours.'"[13] Networking with a fellow indie filmmaker who uses the same producer, Neil Kopp, and the same sound designer, Leslie Shatz, is yet another way Reichardt keeps costs controlled. This frugality drives Reichardt's filming techniques and contributes to her aesthetic.

NEO-NEOREALISM

Reichardt's aesthetic, closely linked to 1940s Italian neorealism, is used in *Wendy and Lucy* to expose social injustice and the socioeconomic issues affecting the working-class poor. In several interviews, Reichardt discusses how her influences inspired the focus of her film. "We [Reichardt and Raymond] were watching a lot of Italian Neorealism and thinking the themes of those films seem to ring true for life in America in the Bush years," she explains to Van Sant.[14] She returns to the film's influences in another interview, stating: "[W]e definitely went back to neorealism, since many of those themes seemed so relevant at the time: the unions, the depression and so on."[15] Reichardt explores what happens to people when they seemingly hold no value to society, a theme from many of the Italian neorealist films. Wendy, like many in Italy after World War II who were jobless, desperately wants to find work, but until she gets to Alaska she is a "blight" on those around her, as Reichardt explains: "In [Italian neorealist] films there's the theme of certain people not being of any use to society—maybe they're too old or poor so they're a blight—they're like stray dogs."[16] Homelessness, poverty, and social rejection are just some of the parallels between Reichardt's film and Vittorio De Sica's 1952 *Umberto D*, and while they have similar messages, it is the emotional impact and intensity of the endings that stands out. The open ending of Reichardt's film leaves spectators space to decide for themselves whether Wendy is a "blight" on society, or whether her struggles will elevate her economic situation. Umberto, however, seems to have exhausted all of his options, and much like Wendy in her train car, as he walks away with his dog Flike, viewers wonder how they will survive. When asked about the inception of her film during a New York Film festival interview and in *Bomb* magazine, Reichardt interweaves struggles between capitalism and environmentalism to explain:

the seeds of the story came about right after [2005 Hurricane] Katrina . . .
after hearing talk about people pulling themselves up by their bootstraps,

and hearing the presumption that people's lives were so precarious due to some laziness on their part. In the country, poverty isn't something you just ignore anymore. There is a real disdain for it . . . we imagined Wendy as a renter; no insurance, just making ends meet, and a fire occurs due to no fault of her own and she loses her place to live. We don't know her back story in the film but we imagined Wendy was in that kind of predicament.[17]

In Sica's *Bicycle Thieves*, Antonio Ricci is in a similar predicament—deemed valueless by society until finding a job—one that requires transportation. He reacquires his pawned bike, only for it to be stolen. He, like Wendy, loses himself through unethical behavior, although Wendy does not seem as vexed about her decision to steal dog food as Ricci does about stealing a bike; after all, the stakes for the victim of a stolen bike in 1940s Italy are much higher. Reichardt explains that she was revisiting and influenced by the New German cinema and the British Angry Young Man films as well as the Italians: "films that were rooted in issues of class and whose heroes are confronted with difficult situations that often seem beyond their control."[18] While spectators feel sympathy for Ricci, Reichardt believes Americans who live in an abundant society, unlike Italians after World War II, might have a different take on Wendy: "There was a time when this kind of character would seem heroic, but nowadays there doesn't seem to be too much support in America for any kind of truly alternative lifestyle."[19] This "alternative lifestyle" in reference to *Wendy and Lucy* translates as extreme poverty and homelessness. Reichardt's decision to use neorealist techniques, whether out of economic necessity or not, gives her work a distinctive look. Neorealism allows Reichardt an artistic avenue for political and social expression through form, and as some critics observe, her "volatile alloy of documentary and theatrical elements."[20] This is evident in Reichardt's work as she mixes neorealism with innovative forms such as "slow cinema" and stark minimalism to create distinctive films that command audience engagement and reflection.

Reichardt deploys realism, a tool of dominant ideologies, to show audiences the overlooked or marginalized: women, poor and working-class people, and the homeless. In "Image and Voice: Approaches to Marxist-Feminist Film Criticism," Christine Gledhill discusses Roland Barthes's claim that "Realism . . . produces myth" instead of a reflection of reality, and concludes that technology and form, such as the use of newsreel footage, can be just as important as content (or even more so) in determining how realistic audiences perceive a film to be.[21] D. W. Griffith found that mixing a representation of history with fiction in *Birth of a Nation* (1915) gave the illusion of reality, and Gledhill underscores this: "Realism, as a particular mode, depends on adherence to historically specific conventions that 'signify' (rather than 'reflect') reality."[22] With this in mind, filmmakers perpetuate or "signify" patriarchal and capitalist agendas, knowingly or not, because "the realistic image of the world is not a simple reflection of real life but a highly mediated production of cinematic practice."[23] If this means all representations of reality are really "myth" and a "production" instead of a reflection, subversive filming techniques and content are central to obtaining alternative versions of reality. Gledhill suggests that neo-Marxism "changes the projection of criticism from the discovery of meaning to that of uncovering the means of its production."[24]

In the 1995 interview with *Bomb* magazine, Todd Haynes asked Reichardt whether "truth in movies motivated" her and she replied: "I do like realism in the movies—just not to the point where you aren't sure why you're at the movies."[25] Reichardt uses a realistic aesthetic to subversively deconstruct patriarchal and capitalist agendas. While her use of narrative deconstruction varies, her films work in a seamless way, without drawing attention to the act of filming, and instead ask spectators to read into her contradictions. One example of these contradictions is the choice to cast a well-known star, Michelle Williams, to represent a lower-class woman tumbling toward homelessness. Williams portrays an "everywoman" who buys into the capitalist ideology that leads to extreme poverty, and whose storyline allows Reichardt an opportunity to address the economic downturn affecting many Americans at the time the film was released in 2008.

Kelly Reichardt's work subtly but effectively exposes capitalist ideologies using a female-centered narrative, "neo-neorealism," and socioeconomically conscious content. Gledhill quotes Jean-Luc Godard, director of *Breathless* (1960), in asserting that a filmmaker's job is "not to reflect reality but to expose the reality of the reflection" and in so doing subvert the normalizing effect that capitalism and patriarchal culture impose on art through their "construction of reality."[26] In *Wendy and Lucy*, Reichardt reflects a picture of social realities for the American working class and poor in the wake of unexpected widespread natural devastation, such as the effects of Hurricane Katrina; without savings or insurance the homeless and lower working classes were unable to recover, reinforcing that for them the "American Dream" is a myth. In both versions of the narrative, Raymond's short story and Reichardt's film adaptation, Wendy is unable to get back on her feet after an unexpected material loss in her hometown of Muncie, Indiana. Like many Americans teetering toward homelessness, Wendy has bought into the idea of an American Dream that is unobtainable.

In her adaptation Reichardt leaves out the expositional dialogue in Raymond's short story that would explain Wendy's prior situation and current contemplations, so audiences rely on Michelle Williams's body language and inferences. In an interview Reichardt observes that "there is so much internal about her" when referring to Williams's style of acting. Viewers are left to guess at Wendy's thoughts, while Raymond's readers get narration concerning the American Dream she thinks will be one step closer once she arrives in Alaska to work: "[Wendy] refused to let the fantasy get any larger than that. The notion of actually getting ahead was not even worth contemplating. All she hoped for was firm ground under her feet. The dream of a house with a fenced-in yard and rosebushes would wait for another time."[27] Raymond's words, more hopeful in tone, correlate to the opening scene of the film as Wendy and Lucy walk together and play. At the end of the story and the film, however, Wendy chooses to say goodbye to her dog, since Lucy is closer than Wendy to achieving a stable life in her foster home. This is one example of how both artists examine a crippling neoliberal economy and a capitalism that marginalizes poor populations. Wendy wants the house with a picket fence, and this fantasy serves the patriarchal and capitalist bottom line, but in reality, as shown in Reichardt's film when Wendy tearfully lets Lucy stay at her new home, these dreams are not only myths for many working-class people (such as Wally), but contribute to their poverty. In Raymond's short story, Wendy ties her missteps to consumerism: "Somewhere, she knew, she has gone wrong, but for the life of her she couldn't tell where. Images of her new couch—destroyed by the flood—plagued her, and she tried to banish them from her mind."[28] While viewers never receive this backstory in the film, it is an easily imagined scenario for many. Toward the beginning of the short story Wendy mentions wanting to pay off her Visa card, indicating that like many Americans she has worked low-wage jobs, lived hand to mouth, and bought the capitalist vision of "having it all" by putting purchases on credit. If disaster strikes in any form, working-class poor people like Wendy have no economic safety net. It is in the final scene with the mechanic, Bill, as he is explaining her car cannot be fixed, that audiences see this realization hit Wendy (Figure 6.1). She stands listening to his technical explanation, eyes wide at first in anger, then denial, and finally after he takes a phone call, allowing her a moment to turn away and fully grasp the situation, defeat. With a few sentences, Raymond says what Reichardt is working to convey in body language: that consumerism and the mythical American dream have begun Wendy's spiral into homelessness.

GENDER AND THE NARRATIVE OF HOMELESSNESS

Wendy and Lucy makes spectators grapple with the stereotypes and realities of being homeless in America. Reichardt's stark neorealistic style tells a hidden story of homeless women, one that contradicts stereotypes of the homeless population as black, Hispanic, or mentally unstable. As pointed out by Michael Sicinski in his review of *Wendy and Lucy* for *Cineaste*, Wendy does not display the stereotypical identifying characteristics of homelessness. She is Caucasian and does not have dirt under her fingernails, stained clothing, or

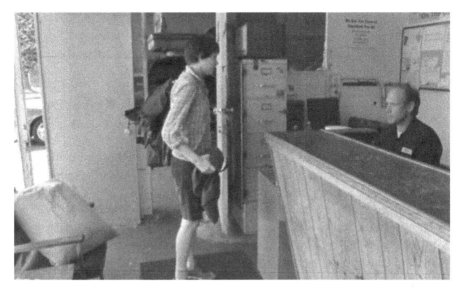

Figure 6.1 Wendy and the mechanic

blackened or missing teeth. Sicinski asks whether Raymond and Reichardt are proposing two unreconciled images of Wendy, the "rebellious college student" mixed with the "fashion accoutrements" of the "drifter, tramp, hobo, derelict" to construct a narrative so "an upscale, mostly white bourgeois art-house audience [can] mentally elide [those tropes] during the act of spectatorship."29 Viewers might compare Wendy to a typical college student who is a novice on the streets, as illustrated by her inability to successfully shoplift; but there are many indications that Wendy is not a "rebellious college student" on a road trip. Not only does the opening scene show viewers that becoming a "gutter punk" is a possible future for Wendy, since she too is reduced to train-hopping by the end, but it also creates space for the introduction of Icky (Will Oldham). His inclusion functions to create an expectation or model of the typical Alaskan cannery employee; a college education is not necessary for the labor-intensive work required at the canneries. In addition to the choice of future employment, the fact that Wendy does not have a reliable phone number or an address is a telltale sign that she is not simply a student on a road trip, but instead one misstep away from complete homelessness. She is one of the many women in America who Rose Aguilar, host of the radio show *The Call* and author of a 2013 article on homeless women in *The Nation*, refers to in an interview broadcast on National Public Radio's *Here and Now*:

> You'll notice that 95 percent of [San Francisco's homeless] are men because the streets of San Francisco are far too dangerous for women. And so the women are mostly invisible. And the women that I've found,

they don't 'look homeless.' We've got that media image of that guy on the corner screaming, well these women take good care of themselves. They don't have tattered clothing. They don't smell. They might be riding on a public transportation system sitting next to you and you don't even know it.[30]

According to Aguilar, many homeless women ride all night on buses or find twenty-four-hour coffee shops, because being a homeless woman is very dangerous. After Wendy reluctantly phones her sister and brother-in-law, viewers realize she has no familial support. Her sister, after hearing the Honda has broken down, offers no financial or even emotional support, saying, "What does she want us to do about it? We can't do anything. We're strapped. I don't know what she wants," and then hangs up. One of Aguilar's interviewees, a homeless woman named Susan, had a story particularly reminiscent of Wendy's family disconnect: "I have six children, but I'm not close to them currently. I have lived with my family in the past but it just didn't work out." Susan's comment echoes Wendy's possible thoughts as she faces costly car repairs and walks away from the fruitless family phone call: "You always think it's someone else and when you are in this situation you can't believe it's you and I think you think your family will be there for you and they're not." Wendy's only reliable family is her dog Lucy, and their relationship represents far more than simply companionship.

While not focusing exclusively on homeless women, Ari Shapiro on his radio program *Talk of the Nation* tackled questions about American poverty and homelessness. One female caller, identified as Elbe from San Antonio, Texas, touched on why homeless women need animal companionship:

> I just want to say, when I was homeless, I had a dog. I used my dog as protection because I was just a single young woman on the streets . . . there's a lot of young women that are out on the street that are completely homeless . . . a lot of them have dogs for protection so they don't get raped or murdered or something.[31]

Andy, the young male grocery employee who catches Wendy stealing dog food, like many middle-class Americans does not understand the importance of a dog to homeless women and opines: "If a person can't afford dog food, they shouldn't have a dog!" Elbe's rationalizations for keeping a dog are reinforced by Reichardt when Wendy camps without her dog at the back of a wooded community park. A homeless man (Larry Fessenden) finds Wendy asleep near the train tracks and, after sorting through her pack, wakes her up with his deranged rants. At one point Wendy looks directly up at him and he immediately yells, "Don't look at me." Reichardt forces audiences to lie still with Wendy, eyes shut tight, as he works himself up into a rage, saying: "I'm out here trying to be a good boy, but they won't let me. They've got to know I've killed over 700 people with my bare hands." One loose implication is that he might be a military veteran and is now reduced to homelessness, poverty, and untreated mental illness. In Raymond's short story, the homeless man shares a much more violent and graphic tale and alludes to his veteran status by saying, "We're never going to win this war" and "we lost, man."[32] Not only is Reichardt commenting on the vulnerability of homeless women, but also the high numbers of veterans who are homeless or living in poverty. Viewers leave the scene, like Wendy, shaken and terrified at what could have happened, and wondering what her future might hold without a dog or safe shelter. Reichardt has revealed in interview that she did not see much hope at the end of *Wendy and Lucy*, and in fact Gus Van Sant goes further by saying, "This one [compared to her prior films] has a sense of downward spiral to the point where it's devastating," reflecting the hopelessness and dangers homeless women face on a daily basis.[33]

Reichardt's characterization of Wendy is an effort to broaden viewers' understanding of poverty and homelessness, and in effect offers an alternative to the stereotypical privileged white patriarchal perspective on the poor. Many might argue that Wendy's bad judgments created her precarious position: she decided to drive cross-country in a twenty-year-old car, budgeted no emergency money, opted to travel to Alaska for a job, stole dog food, slept in a park at night, decided against receiving money for aluminum cans, and did not carry a cell phone. However, these so-called choices are a result of economic demands and/or lack of education or family support. When she steals food for Lucy, Wendy's focus is on feeding her family. She is not thinking about repercussions, nor does she seem morally disturbed by stealing from the store, which might reflect the frequency of the act. Either way, there is no trace of "rebellion or a competitive sport,"[34] despite what some critics have indicated, in her approach to finding food. A more focused look at the grocery store debate and a deeper knowledge of the original short story rebuke the idea that Wendy's characterization is crafted to appeal to a "white bourgeois art-house audience."[35] While Reichardt decides not to adapt what would seemingly have been a lengthy shot of Wendy's internal monologue at the grocery store, Jon Raymond in his short story goes into detail about her grocery trip. Through internal narrative readers learn that Wendy prefers to buy in bulk as opposed to single cans, and Reichardt hints at this preference when Wendy pulls a large, empty dog food bag out of her trunk. In the story, she compares prices and ingredients before deciding to steal, indicating that her decision is fueled by logic:

> In the worst-case scenario, she figured, she could always steal food, but that was not the case with such things as gas or car repairs . . . Three cans

Figure 6.2 Wendy handing over the cans

of premium dog food equaled almost two gallons of gas, [Wendy] calculated, which in turn equaled almost fifty miles of road . . . She and Lucy needed just enough to last a matter of days, that was all.[36]

Wendy is prioritizing her safety over food, as do many lower-working-class or homeless women.

Wendy and Lucy not only focuses on the precarious position of the lower working classes and homeless American women, but questions the government's social responsibilities to its citizens. Collecting recyclable items often helps support those in poverty, and Wendy probably has dog food money in mind as she collects cans. During the recycling center scene, she tries to turn in a bag of aluminum cans but is pressured by a man in a wheelchair to leave as the wait is not worth her time, so she reluctantly hands her collection to him (Figure 6.2). In essence, the scene is about assumptions: Wendy is being judged by her appearance, and then pressured by the assumption that she is not in real need and does not belong in an aluminum can recycling line. In this scene, the film illustrates hierarchies within the homeless community and debunks assumptions about authenticity. Wendy occupies a liminal position: she does not match a white patriarchal society's image of homelessness, and even others in the homeless community judge her on this basis. The reality, however, is that the money from those cans might have kept Wendy from stealing dog food, which could have contributed to a more hopeful ending.

SOCIAL REALISM AND THE AT-RISK VS. THE CAN-DO GIRL

While Raymond and Reichardt fault a capitalist society for Wendy's situation, a discussion of individual accountability and judgment might suggest that Wendy should be labeled as an "at-risk girl." In her book *Future Girl: Young Women in the Twenty-first Century*, Anita Harris discusses the socially desirable "can-do girl" in comparison to the undesirable "at-risk girl." The can-do girl is an example of a girl who has professional aspirations and the support structures to attain those goals; she is what many Western countries see as the future of the workforce and an ideal citizen. Harris discusses the many ways can-do girl is monitored so she follows a path toward success, which is symbolized through her ability to purchase and consume.[37] Because Wendy and others like her have no access to technology or social media, they are less easily monitored and conditioned to follow through with the can-do girl ideology of achievement. Capitalist and consumer markets have a strong interest in creating as many can-do girls as possible, and vilifying those who choose or fall into alternative life paths: "the emphasis on the resilience and achievements of young women is matched by a concern, even a moral panic, that at least some of them are not succeeding as they should be . . . The construction of the can-do girls and the remaindering of the others in the at-risk category" are crucial to create and maintain a regulatory system for their behavior.[38] At every turn Wendy is sanctioned by this "regulatory system" for not fitting into American middle-class consumerism, but nowhere more so than in her dealings with Bill, the mechanic. The Honda, her most valuable monetary position, is judged worthless by the standards of a disposable culture, so much so that the option of selling it for scrap metal is never mentioned. As an at-risk girl, Wendy herself becomes disposable when the mechanic suggests a solution to her: "I tell you what, just make it thirty bucks for the tow, for the [pause] to junk it and everything and that will be it." The mechanic is fulfilling a monitoring role in society by establishing that his priority is to make a profit, as hers should be, and he must get her car off his lot to make room for paying customers. In other words, Wendy should give up her Alaskan trip, go home, and fall in line with young women who contribute economically to society. While Andy the grocery store clerk also monitors Wendy's behavior, the interactions between Wendy and Bill illustrate the extreme vulnerability of the lower classes.

As seen in Wendy's case, Harris explains the at-risk girl is one who may have professional aspirations but lacks the support structure to achieve those goals; she may live in a violent neighborhood or an extremely rural one, with parents who are either uneducated about the process of reaching their daughter's goals or have a different vision for her, one that may include working to support the family instead of pursuing further education.[39] Harris notes that since Western governments have a vested interest in creating consumer-oriented, can-do girls with little concern about the effects of constant achievement, the "at-risk girl" is demonized as not having tried hard enough and placing herself in jeopardy resulting from poor choices: "Success and failure are constructed as though they were dependent on strategic effort and good personal choices," and "failure is deemed to be the consequence of an individual limitation . . . it is the idea that good choices, effort, and ambition alone are responsible for success that has come to separate the can-dos from the at-risks."[40] While Reichardt's protagonist qualifies as an at-risk girl because of her rural roots, lack of family support structure, and poor choices, Wendy is a mix of Harris's two categories because she is Caucasian and has delayed motherhood (the latter being one of the characteristics of the can-do girl). Reichardt mixes these qualities in her characterization to create an emotional conflict for audiences who have been conditioned to monitor and regulate girls at risk. Viewers are introduced to the complexity of poverty in America, and instead of faulting individual motivation and accomplishment, they may begin to question their own adherence to a social system that fails an at-risk-girl: "The construction of the at-risk girl serves to house a diversity of marginalized youth whose problems are rarely named as structural."[41] These categories are ultimately created, as Harris indicates, to take focus away from the failures of the social system and place them back on the individual, who typically has few or no options. Whether from the grocery store manager, the police, or the mechanic, viewers keep waiting for Wendy to find assistance, but with Reichardt's neorealistic style, it never happens, and she is forced to leave Lucy and train-hop to Alaska. Reichardt is filming a hauntingly universal story for the underclass of America, especially in the wake of climate change and natural disasters.

ECOFEMINIST CONCERNS

Reichardt interweaves gender and social politics with subtle environmental commentary, while her form highlights feminist concerns. Spectators see through the eyes of a female protagonist, identifying with her fears, anxieties, and loneliness as the camera privileges her point of view. Reichardt uses this combination to voice her social and environmental concerns without being overly didactic, and Wendy's victimization by a neoliberal economy can be analyzed through the lens of ecofeminist theory. Serpil Oppermann defines ecofeminism as "subverting all gendered associations. It sheds light on the complex interconnections of gender, sexuality, ecology, and ideology that have impacts beyond women's bodies."[42] In this context, ecofeminism draws comparisons between social injustice to the pollution and destruction of the environment. It emphasizes the cyclical nature of human connections to each other and to the planet. As Reichardt has explained, the idea for *Wendy and Lucy* stemmed from the devastation of lower-working-class populations after natural disasters; Wendy, according to Raymond's story, has lost everything to flooding. One of the larger implications of the film is the political goal, championed by ecofeminism, of raising the average middle-class American's awareness of the impact capitalist practices have on the lower working classes and the environment. Through her chapter, "Viscous Porosity: Witnessing Katrina," in *Material Feminisms*, Nancy Tuana echoes Reichardt's environmental message in *Wendy and Lucy*:

> As the phenomenon of [Hurricane] Katrina's devastation had taught us all too well, the knowledge that is too often missing and is often desperately needed is at the intersection between things and people . . . between experiences and bodies . . . Katrina then is emblematic of the porosity between humans and our environment, between social practices and natural phenomena.[43]

As Tuana indicates, the consequences of natural disasters include personal disasters and they are inherently linked, illustrating the fragility of the lower classes worldwide and the need for capitalist societies to make changes in consumption to mitigate their destructive impact on the environment.

Each of Reichardt's feature films juxtaposes natural beauty with scenes of environmental exploitation and its consequences, from the development of the Florida Everglades and illegal dumping or urban sprawl in Oregon, to the 1800s rush for land settlements near the Cascade Mountains and dam construction in salmon-inhabited rivers. All of these environments represent a home for their inhabitants, but in *Wendy and Lucy* Reichardt challenges the middle-class understanding of what constitutes a home. The idea or definition of home is also complicated by ecofeminist scholar Greta Gaard in her article "New Directions for Ecofeminism: Toward a More Feminist Ecocriticism." Besides articulating the need for ecocriticism to further acknowledge contributions by feminist ideology, she discusses the similarities between place studies and ecofeminist ecoregionalism, saying that "'place studies' seems to have pre-empted earlier concerns about bioregionalism and the 'nature of home' that have been foundational issues in ecofeminism."[44] Using the historical placement of women in the home, Gaard discusses the potential isolating effect and the "undervaluing" of the domestic sphere by patriarchal culture, since "home" is a place for "women, children, slaves, servants, and nonhuman animals" and "a person's worth is gauged in monetary terms" in the public sphere.[45] In *Wendy and Lucy*, viewers are given a different set of circumstances to grapple with: a woman in the public sphere, with no obvious home and no monetary worth. According to Gaard, "'Home' needs to be understood as 'a set of relationships, a series of contextual experiences,' and a place of connection where one lives physically, where one is emotionally connected, and where one is part of a community of beings."[46] Gaard's resonating message is for material and resource consumers to conceive of the global environment as a shared home in an effort to reduce negative environmental impact.[47] As ecofeminists push for a redefinition of home, Gaard's ideology applies to the meaning of home in *Wendy and Lucy.* Using Gaard's definition of home, Wendy becomes homeless firstly by losing her apartment through natural causes; secondly by losing Lucy, who acts as her home in the sense of emotional investment and connection; and thirdly by losing her car, which is the last signifier of value to the "community of [consumer] beings." Traditional vestiges of home are represented during Wendy's payphone conversation with her sister immediately after she loses Lucy. It is clear that Wendy lacks a family home with her sister and brother-in-law, and there is no parallel scene in Raymond's short story of the payphone exchange, suggesting that Reichardt wants to highlight Wendy's lack of options as well as her loss of support or access to any traditional home. Instead of a payphone scene, Raymond addresses Wendy's loss (as interpreted through Gaard's definition of home as "a community of beings") with his description of her reaction to the cost of the car repair: "Overhead, the lights seemed to flutter, and for a moment she worried the whole world might disappear. But in fact nothing happened; the world remained as it was . . . Her problems had no discernible effect on anything beyond herself whatsoever."[48] Wendy feels outside of any community, and her isolation is enhanced by the stoicism projected by Williams after the payphone and mechanic scenes. In both cases, Williams is tense and motionless with no emotional outbursts, giving her spiral into complete homelessness an almost tangible weight.

By opting to adapt a short story about the effects of capitalism on the poor and adding environmental elements connecting consumerism to natural disasters, Reichardt uses narrative to sustain an audience's emotional involvement in a way that news clips covering disasters are incapable of achieving. Her film seeks to overcome the "materializ[ation] [of] ignorance" that existed before and shortly after life-altering storms such as Hurricane Katrina, as Tuana explains:

> the poverty Katrina forced us to witness came as a 'shock' to the nation as it watched news coverage of Katrina's wake. This serves as an interesting lens for considering some of the ways that ignorance is materialized and the various institutions and motives that have a stake in the production and maintenance of ignorance.[49]

Tuana insinuates that ignorance about Americans in poverty serves corporate interests, since maintaining an illusion of economic status quo encourages middle-class spending. In interviews, Reichardt agrees with ecofeminists' agenda, stating that "[t]here's political in the personal," and this creates a need for "restructuring power and challenging unequal power relationships [with] the goal of transforming economic, political, and institutional structures . . . for the defense of threatened areas and oppressed groups [with an agreement that] there is no separating the personal from the political."[50] *Wendy and Lucy* supports this agenda by reminding viewers who the "oppressed groups" are and how quickly they fade from memory after disaster strikes, as the following editorial from the 19 September 2005 issue of *Newsweek* notes:

> It takes a hurricane. It takes a catastrophe like Katrina to strip away the old evasions, hypocrisies and not-so-benign neglect . . . For the moment, at least, Americans are ready to fix their restless gaze on enduring problems of poverty, race, and class that have escaped their attention. Does this mean a new war on poverty? No, especially with Katrina's gargantuan price tag.[51]

The fragmented account of events presented by documentaries and news programs can distance viewers from a tragedy, especially one involving large numbers of victims; however, Reichardt's use of a narrative instead of photography, documentary, or news clips keeps audiences fully present and invested in Wendy's plight. Gus Van Sant describes how the film's narrative about poverty resonated with him: "After watching *Wendy and Lucy*, it [realization of poverty's effects] was just palpable. It was so omnipresent. I was part of the film, but the film had stopped . . . It's a delicate thing to get somebody into a feeling that they can't actually get rid of right away."[52] By using a narrative format to depict her characters' situations, Reichardt keeps poverty and survival in the forefront of audiences' minds long after viewing the film.

The ability of audiences and critics to broaden their perspectives concerning homelessness is key to Reichardt's agenda, as she explains in a 2008 interview with *Artforum*: "I think of [*Wendy and Lucy*] as being shot in 'ugly America'— it's a beige film, full of flat, anonymous walls that were difficult to deal with."[53] This style creates a claustrophobic effect, allowing spectators to empathize with Wendy's trapped situation. While the entire film voices concern for those in poverty, a discussion between Wendy and Wally reflects the fears and frustrations experienced by Americans during the US housing crisis that began in early 2008 and cost thousands of Americans their homes and livelihoods. In an unprecedented move, the Bush administration subsidized the private and governmental agencies that made housing loans or financed risky mortgages in an effort to stabilize the economy. Many blamed these banks and organizations for the economic downturn; but according to the *Journal of Business Inquiry*, "the primary cause of the recession was the credit crisis resulting from the bursting of the housing bubble."[54] While trust in government support teetered, trust in private corporations and economic systems such as the markets was lost. The resulting fear, lack of trust, and frustration with a jobless economy is articulated as Wendy sits beside Wally, the Walgreen's security guard, discussing the decline of jobs in the area and the widening gap between economic classes:

> Wendy: Not a lot of jobs around here, are there?
> Wally: I'll say I don't know what the people do all day. Used to be a mill, but that's been closed a long time now.
> Wendy: You can't get a job without an address anyway, or a phone.
> Wally: You can't get an address without an address. You can't get a job without a job. It's all fixed.

When Wally implies that the system is "fixed," he is referring directly to corporate greed and capitalist mentalities as a reason why lower-working-class and poverty-stricken Americans cannot improve their economic status or secure a job. Reichardt has created two "every person" characters, and in this scene, as they discuss the key themes of the film, audiences clearly hear Raymond and Reichardt's own frustration with the government's inability to support its citizens.

While *Wendy and Lucy* does not highlight a working-class woman's struggle to feed and shelter her children, as do films such as Courtney Hunt's *Frozen River* (2008) or Debra Granik's *Winter's Bone* (2010), it is a similar story of struggle and sacrifice. Reichardt makes the care of a dog, rather than children, central to her plot while still focusing on "the terrible effects of a neoliberal capitalism [that] have become much more visible and tangible."[55] In her book *Not Hollywood: Independent Film at the Twilight of the American Dream*, Sherry Ortner discusses the vulnerability of America's working class and echoes Reichardt's and other female filmmakers' concerns: "The point about people in lower-class positions . . . is not just that they're poor—have less money, less things—but that their lives are much more insecure. They have less margin of error and are much closer to some edge where their lives may start coming apart."[56] By focusing on class structure, *Wendy and Lucy* speaks to the financial fears of middle-class American women as discussed by Ortner:

> For many Americans, then, the working class can never be totally Other, or at least, it is always part Other and part self. Unlike most Others, working-class figures thus create very powerful possibilities for identification and disidentification . . . these films can be read as telling stories about the implications of the contemporary neoliberal economy not only for poor women but for many middle-class women who face the specter of downward mobility for themselves and their children.[57]

Contemporary women's films that focus on poverty and female struggle use class issues as an equalizer as well as an attempt to illuminate poor women's struggles. By using neo-neorealism and a minimalist aesthetic, Reichardt confronts the damage done by a neoliberal economy and mirrors a possible reality for many middle-class women who would prefer to keep this depiction of the Other an impossibility. She differs from her contemporaries, however, by depicting a lower-class woman sinking deeper into poverty with little to no hope, while Granik and Hunt end with a glimmer of hope for their female protagonists. The emphasis on consumer goods in *Wendy and Lucy*, such as the Honda and the dog food, reflects the post-feminist concerns that consumerism gives power to women and a middle-class fear of that lack of power: "the loss of the ability to shop and consume is seen as one of the worst imaginable fates for a middle-class woman."[58] In Granik and Hunt's films the female protagonists find a way to perpetuate this post-feminist version of power, securing their purchases; Wendy, however, not only fails at keeping her home but also loses her "child" in the process. This type of open ending, Ortner points out, illustrates that "people in the lower levels of society can always drop down even lower, with even more disastrous effects," and when Wendy begins her slow economic descent the film "creates even more powerful images of the potential devastation of downward mobility" for middle-class audiences.[59] While Ortner reads these films as "allegories of the potential fate of any women in the new social order, in which neoliberal policies, greater likelihood of divorce, and various patriarchal biases combine to render women particularly vulnerable to downward mobility," they also represent an effort to define a new style or representation of feminist politics.[60] Reichardt and many of her contemporary female filmmakers shy away from officially declaring themselves feminists, as do many women who use post-feminist concerns to define their ideology. Ortner discusses Mary Harron (*Anna Nicole*, 2013), who, like Reichardt, disassociates herself from the feminist filmmaker label and claims not to have a political agenda. This type of post-feminism is explained by Ortner as a lack of organizational structure for third wave feminism, which the second wave depended upon:

> In that sense they [female-directed films] are indeed 'post-feminist,' that is, they have absorbed the concerns of the feminist movement and to some degree take them for granted. But this does not mean that the filmmakers do not see—and represent—the continuing urgency of those concerns in the contemporary world.[61]

In keeping with a trend in independent women's films of raising awareness through telling marginalized women's stories, Reichardt highlights women's concerns in all her films but refuses to offer lasting political or social solutions, possibly to avoid didacticism. While both Granik and Hunt present audiences with more hopeful endings than the one in Reichardt's film, they offer no sustainable paths for their protagonists, who will continue to feed and provide safety and shelter for themselves and their families.

Through raising public awareness with *Wendy and Lucy*, Reichardt criticizes a government that allows private markets to wreak havoc on working class and poor populations. Ultimately Wendy is unable to maintain society's economic or behavioral expectations of the can-do girl, and so is deemed disposable. Her downward spiral into homelessness with no safety net, family or financial, is only one of many American life stories since the environmental and economic disasters of the mid-2000s. Reichardt's choice to highlight American women's experience of poverty through Wendy creates a non-didactic space in which spectators can revise their understanding of homelessness, and demonstrates how from an ecofeminist point of view all Americans should share a measure of accountability. Her critique of American values as they relate to women and the environment continues in her 2010 film *Meek's Cutoff*, in which *Wendy and Lucy*'s concern with environmental and political crisis is subtly shifted back to the nineteenth-century debate around manifest destiny and its effects on the landscape and native peoples.

NOTES

1. "*Wendy and Lucy* (2008): Awards," *Internet Movie Database*, <http://www.imdb.com/title/tt1152850/awards?ref_=tt_awd> (accessed 20 September 2017).
2. "*Wendy and Lucy*," *Box Office Mojo*, <http://www.boxofficemojo.com/movies/?id=wendyandlucy.htm> (accessed 20 September 2017).
3. Reichardt quoted in David Liu, "In Conversation: Kelly Reichardt," *Kino Obscura*, 20 August 2012, <http://kino-obscura.com/post/30205580824/in-conversation-kelly-reichardt> (accessed 20 September 2017).
4. Ibid.
5. Ibid.
6. Reichardt quoted in Brian Sholis, "Interview with Kelly Reichardt," *Artforum*, October 2008, <https://www.artforum.com/inprint/issue=200808&id=21124> (accessed 20 September 2017).
7. Doris Toumarkine, "Lab Results: Oscilloscope Tests Today's Market With Cost-Effective Strategies," *Film Journal International* 112, no.10 (2009): 10.
8. Reichardt quoted in Gus Van Sant, "Artists in Conversation: Kelly Reichardt," *Bomb* 105 (2008): 81, <http://bombmagazine.org/article/3182/kelly-reichardt> (accessed 20 September 2017).
9. Ibid.
10. Reichardt quoted in Sholis, "Interview."
11. Michelle Williams quoted in "Wendy and Lucy Q&A: Kelly Reichardt and Michelle Williams," *Filmlinc.com*, 4 October 2008.
12. Reichardt quoted in Liu, "In Conversation."

13. Ibid.
14. Reichardt quoted in Van Sant, "Artists in Conversation," p. 78.
15. Reichardt quoted in Liu, "In Conversation."
16. Reichardt quoted in Van Sant, "Artists in Conversation," p. 78.
17. Ibid.
18. Reichardt quoted in Sholis, "Interview."
19. Ibid.
20. A. O. Scott, "Neo Neo Realism," *The New York Times*, 22 March 2009: A38.
21. Christine Gledhill, "Image and Voice: Approaches to Marxist-Feminist Film Criticism," in Diane Carson et al. (eds.), *Multiple Voices in Feminist Film Criticism* (Minneapolis: Minnesota University Press, 1994), p. 114.
22. Ibid. p. 113.
23. Ibid.
24. Ibid. p. 114.
25. Reichardt quoted in Van Sant, "Artists in Conversation," p. 78.
26. Gledhill, "Image and Voice," p. 115.
27. Jon Raymond, "Train Choir," in *Livability* (New York: Bloomsbury, 2009), p. 217.
28. Ibid. pp. 242–3.
29. Michael Sicinski, "*Wendy and Lucy*," *Cineaste* (2009), <https://www.cineaste.com/spring2009/wendy-and-lucy> (accessed 20 September 2017).
30. Rose Aguilar interviewed by Robin Young, *Here and Now*, National Public Radio, 25 February 2013.
31. "Elbe" interviewed by Ari Shapiro, *Talk of The Nation*, National Public Radio, 6 December 2012.
32. Raymond, "Train Choir," p. 246.
33. Van Sant, "Artists in Conversation," p. 78.
34. Sicinski, "*Wendy and Lucy*."
35. Ibid.
36. Raymond, "Train Choir," pp. 217–18.
37. Anita Harris, *Future Girl: Young Women in the Twenty-first Century* (New York: Routledge, 2004), p. 21.
38. Ibid. p. 16.
39. Ibid. pp. 26–7.
40. Ibid. p. 32, p. 15.
41. Ibid. p. 35.
42. Serpil Oppermann, "Feminist Ecocriticism: The New Ecofeminist Settlement," *Feminismo/s: Special Issue on Ecofeminism* (2013): 2–3.
43. Nancy Tuana, "Viscous Porosity: Witnessing Katrina," in Stacy Alaimo and Susan Hekman (eds.), *Material Feminism* (Bloomington: Indiana University Press, 2008), p. 189, p. 193.
44. Greta Gaard, "New Directions for Ecofeminism: Toward a More Feminist Ecocriticism," *Interdisciplinary Studies in Literature and Environment* 17, no. 4 (2010): 654.
45. Ibid. p. 655.
46. Ibid. p. 656.
47. Ibid.
48. Raymond, "Train Choir," p. 253.
49. Tuana, "Viscous Porosity," p. 203.
50. Ryan Stewart, "Redefining Success: An Interview with Kelly Reichardt," *Slant Magazine*, 5 December 2008, <https://www.slantmagazine.com/features/article/

redefining-success-an-interview-with-kelly-reichardt> (accessed 20 September 2017); Gaard, "New Directions for Ecofeminism," p. 656.
51. Jonathan Alter quoted in Tuana, "Viscous Porosity," p. 204.
52. Van Sant, "Artists in Conversation," p. 78.
53. Reichardt quoted in Sholis, "Interview."
54. Jeff Holt, "A Summary of the Primary Causes of the Housing Bubble and the Resulting Credit Crisis: A Non-Technical Paper," *The Journal of Business Inquiry* (2009): 120.
55. Sherry Ortner, *Not Hollywood: Independent Film at the Twilight of the American Dream* (Durham, NC: Duke University Press, 2013), p. 194.
56. Ibid.
57. Ibid. p. 190.
58. Ibid. p. 195.
59. Ibid. p. 194.
60. Ibid. pp. 197–8.
61. Ibid. p. 195.

CHAPTER 7

Expectations: *Meek's Cutoff*

Is he ignorant or is he just plain evil? That's my quandary. It's impossible to know.—Emily, *Meek's Cutoff*

Based on true events in the history of the Oregon Trail, Kelly Reichardt's fourth feature, *Meek's Cutoff* (2010), is a story of survival, endurance, and trust. The film offers a female perspective of settling the American West, from mundane daily tasks to extraordinary and frightening encounters. Highlighting otherness as an issue, Reichardt interweaves issues of race, leadership, community, and gender into her film, which is based on historical accounts of Oregon's infamous "Terrible Trail." Set in 1845, the film follows the difficult journey of immigrants in search of homesteads. Stephen Meek (Bruce Greenwood) convinces a group of pioneers to take a supposedly safer and shorter route through the Oregon desert, and audiences join the caravan just as the travelers realize they are lost. When Meek and Solomon Tetherow (Will Paton) capture a Cayuse tribesman (Rob Rondeaux), it is Emily Tetherow (Michelle Williams) who ultimately assumes leadership, confronts Meek, and establishes trust in their Cayuse guide. Reichardt offers a subversive allegory by questioning representations of traditional genre, style, and content; her feminist Western is presented in a "slow cinema" style, with political and social content that connects history to the present day. By exploring the cinematic decisions involved in creating an alternative Western, including the choice of a square aspect ratio, slow pacing, and an open narrative structure, *Meek's Cutoff* offers spectators a feminist variant on the form and content of the classical Western.

THE REAL STORY OF MEEK

Kelly Reichardt again engaged Jon Raymond's talents for *Meek's Cutoff*, but instead of co-writing an adaptation of one of his stories (as with *Old Joy* and *Wendy and Lucy*), Reichardt jokes that Raymond got a jump start on her:

> [Raymond] selfishly, selfishly, went directly to the script . . . I'm usually figuring out how to shoot during the process of adapting his short stories into screenplays, but this time he really screwed me on that. And as much as I love the voices Jon created for the nine characters . . . the heart of things rests almost completely outside the dialogue.[1]

Raymond rediscovered the true story of "The Terrible Trail" as he was conducting research for a development company in Bend, Oregon. His employers wanted local historical names for branding golf courses and properties, and that inspired his work on the screenplay. In several interviews both Raymond and Reichardt discuss how the "infamous episode of the early Oregon Trail" inspired the film.[2] Stephen Meek (1808–86) was the younger brother of Joe Meek, a highly successful mountain man and governor of the Oregon territory.[3] Stephen Meek lived in his brother's shadow and hoped to gain fame of his own by leading Solomon Tetherow and 1,000 to 1,500 other immigrants on a shortcut from "Fort Boise, Idaho, to across the center of Oregon Country to the plentiful Willamette Valley, thus avoiding the hostile Cayuse and Walla Walla Indians on the tried route that led northwest into the Blue Mountains and along the Columbia River to the Dalles settlement."[4] Instead the company became lost and, as they do in the film, captured a Native American, offering him a blanket in exchange for guidance out of the desert.[5] Historical accounts show that Meek then deserted the caravan along with his "young bride," causing more than forty deaths and making it "the worst disaster to befall the pioneers who set out for California or Oregon."[6]

PRODUCTION

Even as she was making her breakthrough film *Wendy and Lucy*, Reichardt was researching and planning *Meek's Cutoff* by "reading . . . journals from people who made the journey west."[7] With a two-million-dollar budget, it was a film unlike any she had previously attempted in terms of sheer size and scope: "The cost of feeding the oxen and horses on *Meek's Cutoff* was equal to the entire budget of Reichardt's second film [*Old Joy*]."[8] The film was her most expensive project yet, and even with careful budgeting, it lost money.[9] While some academics and many critics wrote extensively about it, its loss of profit was due to a lack of commercial appeal. According to the website Box Office Mojo, *Meek's Cutoff* made approximately $1,205,257 worldwide (domestic gross $977,772), with the widest release domestically at forty-five theaters.[10] Compared to *Wendy and Lucy*, *Meek's Cutoff* was a commercial risk. Domestically, it was shown in only five more theaters, and stayed in theaters for one week less than *Wendy and Lucy*.[11] There was a predictable box-office boost from the UK with a gross total of $191,882 since Shirley Henderson, a popular British actress, played Glory White; but the increase in ticket sales did not make up for a discrepancy of close to a million dollars.

Meek's Cutoff seemingly breaks Reichardt's unwritten minimalist filmmaking production rules, in that it is a period piece set in the Oregon desert with thirty to fifty crew members, animals, and a child actor. Nevertheless, in other ways it is directly in line with her artistic vision and independent philosophy. After all, a two-million-dollar filming budget is a drop in the bucket for most Hollywood films with stars like Michelle Williams. When Reichardt talked artistic control with *The Guardian*, she repeated her independent ethos: "The more money you take, the more hands there are in the pie . . . Right now, there's no one telling me what to do. I can edit on my own schedule. No one gives me notes outside the same friends who I've been showing my films to since I started"; these friends included executive producers Phil Morrison (*Junebug*, 2005) and Todd Haynes (*I'm Not There*, 2007), the latter of whom she has worked with regularly since *River of Grass*.[12] Other production members from earlier films who worked on *Meek's Cutoff* were Neil Kopp and Filmscience's Anish Savjani. When asked specifically about their roles, Reichardt joked that an additional job for them on this film was to dig "vehicles out of many piles of sand," but other than that, she went on to explain: "Both were with the film the whole time, and there is overlap, but for the most part, Neil is preproduction and production, they are together on post, and then Anish takes the helm for all that comes next."[13]

Evenstar Films and Harmony/Primitive Nero production companies were new additions to her team, but her American distributor, Oscilloscope Laboratories, was not. Considering how successful *Wendy and Lucy* had been for Oscilloscope, the company's decision to be Reichardt's domestic distributor was easy. Reviewing the team that helped release and distribute the picture, it is clear that Reichardt needed a much larger crew in all areas. Soda Pictures, a UK distributor, signed up to market and distribute the film; and Cinetic Media, a New York-based financing company which specializes in connecting producers to financers, was brought on board to help with the "intersection of financing and distribution."[14] Reichardt also engaged historical consultants, animal handlers, an on-set teacher for Tommy Nelson, and composer Jeff Grace, who supplied the exquisitely eerie cello melodies heard throughout the film. Despite the extra investors, production and distribution companies, and seven executive producers, Reichardt once again made a film following her philosophy: independent, artistic, and private.

Meek's Cutoff premiered in September 2010 at the 67th Venice Film Festival before heading to the Toronto, New York, and Sundance Film Festivals. It was nominated for six awards, winning best director at the Gijon International Film Festival, the SIGNIS Award at the Venice Film Festival, and best producer at the Independent Spirit Awards.[15]

While location scouting for the film Reichardt and Kopp decided to opt for the aesthetic appeal and authenticity of the deserts surrounding Burns, Oregon, even though their second choice of Marfa, Texas would have been more convenient in every way, with "FedEx, good food, access to everything you need. Clearly a more practical place to make the movie."[16] To educate and prepare the actors, Reichardt asked them to attend training prior to filming: "The actors all came out a week before shooting for what we called Pioneer Camp. There they learned how to start a fire without matches, how to fire a gun, pitch a tent, cook in the ground, load a wagon and most importantly how to drive the oxen."[17] However, the actors and crew, occupying thirty-two rooms at the Horseshoe Inn, were far more comfortable than historical pioneers, who had to sleep under their wagons. Reichardt has said of her experience working with a larger crew: "I always had a fear of working with a bigger crew and on some days, when we had the stunt people there and all, it was a crew of fifty, but when everybody's really good at their jobs, it doesn't really matter what the size of the crew is."[18] The crew did dwindle to five when she was unable to capture the original ending of the film during the shoot:

> I would like it so that, if the sun's going to set, you're not going home without the ending of your movie . . . [But that's] basically what happened to us: The sun went down, everyone was leaving the next day, and we couldn't afford the animals another day. So a new ending had to be constructed. Michelle, Rod, and I went back with a five-person crew and shot it.[19]

That ending illustrates Reichardt's penchant for framing images in *Meek's Cutoff.* Instead of a conventional closed ending with all narrative questions answered, the audience sees Emily Tetherow's face framed by tree limbs as her doubt-filled gaze rests on their Native American guide, the only hope for her caravan's survival. The ending illustrates Reichardt's ability, while operating on a small budget, to realize artistic decisions that defy the traditional genre conventions associated with the classical Hollywood Western.

SOUND

Creating the right mix of sound and silence was another challenge, Reichardt explains: "A soundscape this quiet was so much harder than what we've done in my other films. There's nothing to hide behind. You hear every mic bump, every hiccup. It's actually really layered, the sound design, but it's very quiet, and that was much harder to mix."[20] During production Reichardt worked with Felix Andrew to capture as much sound as possible, but this proved overwhelming: "he mic'd the oxen, he mic'd the wagons— there were mics everywhere. That was a lot to sort out in the editing room, weeding everything out that I wanted, coming up with the sounds, like the wagons' squeaky wheels. Just getting the particular sounds so that the quiet is emphasized." This proved too difficult, so what work had been done for a musical soundtrack using a group from LA (the Sun City Girls) was scratched.[21] Instead Reichardt was introduced to Jeff Grace in New York by Larry Fessenden. "I knew from the beginning that I wanted wind instruments because the Cayuse were flute players," she recalls—but she was concerned about the soundtrack sounding like a new age album, and in previous films she had generally opted for on-location natural soundtracks instead of musical scores.[22] Grace's score for *Meek's Cutoff* effectively employs instruments that complement the narrative; a beautiful but ominous cello and flute melody highlights the growing distance between each character. The longer the caravan is lost in the desert, the more individually isolated the characters become. The intermittent melody contributes to the oppressive atmosphere, and the pioneers' squeaky wagon wheel represents their plight. Each time viewers hear the squeaks, they know the trancelike march is beginning again. The cello melody accompanied by the hollow flute sound symbolizes the characters' unvoiced questions, and their worry-etched faces remind spectators that the caravan members might not survive their journey.

Silence and muffled discussions create a secondary score for the film; Reichardt has commented on the silence, saying, "I feel like a lot is being said all the time, it's just not in dialogue . . . I was hoping that the rawness of the land would work for how completely raw they are at this point in the journey, worn down to the point of barely being able to have a conversation."[23] Reichardt's use of silence mixed with a minimalist soundtrack is effective, but it is her play with volume that invites audiences to be active and engaged. In an effort to place spectators in the pioneer women's shoes, Reichardt intentionally distances the camera and muffles the dialogue of the men's meetings, frustrating but also engaging viewers: "Usually when you're making a film you expect the camera to be on the person who is doing the talking. In the case of *Meek's Cutoff*, the men are doing a lot of the talking. So yeah, there was some tension at times and it emphasized the assumption of power both on film and in life."[24]

Turning up the volume does not help decipher the words, as spectators are only allowed to hear key phrases as if standing on a ridge, collecting firewood with the ever-busy women. Besides the distant, muffled sound of men's conversations and the clicking of bundled sticks, Reichardt uses the crackling of fire, the kneading of dough, the grinding of coffee beans, the clatter of utensils on tin plates, and the crashes of weighty but beloved objects tossed out the back openings of wagons to remind viewers of the daily chores and rising anxiety felt by the pioneer women.

While the women's fears and concerns are ever-present, they are not painted as victims; instead they are well-rounded characters who are afforded a range of experiences, from playful to victorious. One scene that seems to melt the women's anxiety and silence is when Glory White tells the only joke in the film, as the group sits around a camp fire finishing their dwindling rations. The camera is focused on Glory's husband and son, so spectators are unsure if Glory is sobbing or laughing as she jokes about being jealous of pigs, but either way the outpouring of emotion is jarring in the stoic and restrained narrative: "I'm just thinking of my father's pigs back home, all safe and warm in their beds." After the second muffled sound from Glory, viewers realize she is genuinely laughing and in what seems like an unguarded moment, Glory and Emily turn toward each other, lock eyes, and begin chuckling. The first and only full, broad smile of the film spreads across Emily's face and as she looks up past the camera (maybe at Reichardt), the audience feels a release from the extreme tension that is pervasive throughout the film. The joke, however, has a back story, as Michelle Williams explains: "I was actually reading in the women's journals, and I came across a joke. I showed it to Kelly, and I said, 'Can I say this? Look at this! It's amazing!' And she goes, 'Whoa, yeah, Michelle, that's incredible.' And she puts it in the movie—and she gives it to another character."[25] While Williams seems playfully upset about losing those lines, her research adds more angles to the women's multifaceted experience.

Another playful moment between the women comes during a knitting scene, when the three men are working to fix Thomas Gately's (Paul Dano) broken axle while Meek wanders around camp. Not only does the group work of knitting serve as a common interest (albeit a necessity) among the women, but it shows viewers their unspoken disapproval of Meek as their husbands decide to follow his directions. Reichardt discussed the female bonding she found reflected in the pioneer diaries, as depicted in the knitting scene: "[B]ecause the men had separate chores, people's journals showed how alienating it was between husbands and wives, how the friendships really formed were with the other women on the trail."[26] The women's exchange of sarcastic looks illustrates their mutual trust and agreement about the incompetency of Meek. The looks also reiterate what Emily all but growls at Meek, "You don't know much about women, do you, Stephen Meek?" after he comments that she does not appear to "care for him." Of course his proclamation comes after a disrespectful burp, indicating a saturation of plenty that none of the rest feel, especially while the women's husbands struggle to make repairs in the heat. It also follows on the heels of a racist and sexist comment about "having" Native American women, which evokes an "Oh dear" from Glory. This scene is one of the first to establish Emily's leadership and decision-making abilities, skills she has reluctantly reined in because of gendered social expectations. The smirk from Glory and the feminine "humph" from Emily are all the women are allowed, however, before a stumbling and defensive Meek proclaims, "I know women are different from men; I know that much." He continues with: "Women, women are created on the principle of chaos. The chaos of creation, disorder, bringing new things into the world. Men are created on the principle of destruction—cleansing, order and destruction. Chaos and destruction, the two genders have always had it." Meek's sexist philosophy implies that women need to have order imposed upon them by men, and may need "cleansing" or elimination if they hold radically different beliefs from the mainstream. His comment can be perceived as a veiled threat, since during the last third of the film Meek seems as ready at times to shoot Emily as he is the Cayuse captive. Female viewers may take pleasure in the transfer of power from Meek to Emily, even as he spouts rationalizations about his right to power. In a later, tension-filled "standoff" scene, Meek implies Emily's "Otherness" and need for "cleansing," saying to Solomon, "Looks like your woman got some Indian blood in her, Mr. Teethow." This comment brings out the racial tension threaded throughout the film and serves to connect Meek's associations of the feminine with racial otherness: to him, both are chaotic and in need of white male ordering and, if necessary, cleansing. From the beginning, Emily creates a bond with their captive because, as she explains to Millie, "I want him to owe me something"—and while she holds the same racist assumptions as the other pioneers, she seems capable of identifying and empathizing with others who are marginalized. Meek attempts to remain relevant and remain a force in the group, but is rebuffed by Emily's display of leadership and principles. Despite one interviewer's comment that "Reichardt may not consider herself a feminist filmmaker,"[27] scenes like these submerge audiences in the experience of women settlers.

QUESTIONS OF GENRE: FEMINIST WESTERN

In *Meek's Cutoff* Reichardt requisitions and manipulates the traditional Western further by intentionally keeping the genre label at bay. The description used on the 2010 DVD release of *Meek's Cutoff* calls it "a stark and poetic drama set in 1845," with the word "Western" noticeably missing. In an interview on National Public Radio's *Fresh Air*, moderator Terry Gross points out that the film lacks "any of the things we associate with Westerns—there's no swelling theme music [or] charismatic heroic characters and gunplay and showdowns;" and Reichardt explains that she deliberately never used the term "Western"with her actors.[28] Her admission of disavowing the classical Hollywood Western framework and even labeling the film a drama appears to adhere to Rick Altman's well-known arguments about genre. According to Altman, genre is a process that is ever-shifting and evolving because it is "a record not of the past, but of a living geography, of an ongoing process" that depends on "cultural forces."[29] Genres emerge because the industry is not dealing with a fixed point but instead a process, and so critics' language is ever-changing. Altman cites the first commonly agreed upon Western, Edwin S. Porter's *The Great Train Robbery* (1903), as part of the crime film genre, illustrating how it spawned other crime films, and claiming that the Western did not emerge as a fully fledged genre until much later in the decade.[30] By packaging a film into a neatly theorized and citable category, studios find it easier to market. If it includes such (minimally suggestive) elements as a horse and a Native American, the industry accepts it as a Western and audiences know what to expect. Altman calls this stereotyping the "Producer's Game."[31] The game allows the industry to quickly reproduce films that are successful, and this is one explanation of why many films that might have been better defined as another, or mixed, genre have been marketed as Westerns.[32] Altman suggests that critics have fallen into the "trap" of easy genre categorization.[33] While cinephiles might be frustrated by this capitalist "game," genre expectations are clearly relevant to audience address, and it is precisely thanks to these expectations that Reichardt can subvert traditional Western genre conventions. Furthermore, Reichardt creates awareness of invisible histories or otherness through manipulation of the "game" by using genre-specific Western elements (horses/Native Americans) in her packaging of the film while denying this standard framework by labeling it a drama, and enlarging the image of a female pioneer.

While Reichardt questions and improvises on genre in all her films, she seems to deconstruct the Western particularly thoroughly and incisively via a study of history, the quest narrative, gender, and race. In fact, it is her study of pioneer women's journals and concomitant allegiance to a form of phenomenological realism that explains her creative genre decisions: "[T]here's this trancelike quality about the journey that I haven't really experienced in tales of going west. [I wanted to build] tension by basically not delivering the heightened moment, but working with the way time might have seemed in 1845."[34] It was this experimentation in style and genre that excited scholarly interest in the film, but left mainstream viewers seemingly unsatisfied. Watching *Meek's*

Cutoff, spectators cross into a "non-Hollywood" zone where the experience of time feels very real. Some critics claimed that Reichardt's genre adjustments and pacing created spectator displeasure, calling her film "a chore at times" to watch, which might explain the low box-office turnout. And while others argued that her pacing made the cinematic experience more realistic, many felt obligated to question audience satisfaction:

> It is a bold move for indie favourite Kelly Reichardt to put her own distinctive subtle spin onto the Western genre, and while the presence of the likes of Michelle Williams, Will Patton, Paul Dano and Bruce Greenwood will guarantee respectful reviews it will be tough to find a mainstream audience for her nuanced tale of settlers toughing it out on the Oregon trail.[35]

Reichardt has stated repeatedly that she was not concerned with attracting a wide audience or positive reviews, and felt she was making a film more akin to documentary. "When we were shooting we tried to keep as far away from a man-on-a-horse western as we could . . . it's a desert poem, more *Nanook of the North* than a western."[36] Her particular approach and aesthetics allow for unique genre-bending. Although the film has documentary aspects— Reichardt's use of historical journals to create realist depictions, for instance— it does more than represent the female experience; it stages "what if" scenarios for spectators:

> Making a film like this, you can't help but wonder, would I have made the journey? . . . And then you realize, I wouldn't even have had a choice. My husband would have made the decision. You have to do your politicking at night in the tent, if you can.[37]

An evening tent scene between Solomon and Emily highlights the frustration Reichardt found in pioneer women's diaries. In their tent, after Emily has stood up for her beliefs by threatening Meek at gunpoint, she realizes her husband doubts her judgment:

Solomon: You think he's trustworthy?
Emily: The Indian? I can't say as I do. Just you, that's all.
Solomon: But you're putting your trust in him?
Emily: You're doubtful?
Solomon: I have my doubts.
Emily: What are you thinking, Solomon?
Solomon: I hope Meek hasn't twisted you up, that's all.

A close-up of Emily as her husband get ups and exits the tent shows a stunned, blank expression that turns into a wrinkled brow, and then a struggle to stay composed. This conversation with Solomon suggests that Emily is acting out of uncontained emotion and is putting the group at risk. Clearly Reichardt is making a powerful comment on patriarchal expectations and the limitations of women, not only through the film's content but through its form.

Meek's Cutoff teeters on the edge of experimental cinema in its use of the square screen and traits from slow cinema, strategies which might also be treated as "divergences from genre." One of the most distinctive elements of *Meek's Cutoff* is its aspect ratio of 1:37:1, instead of the more accessible and widely used rectangle or widescreen. Reichardt was advised that by choosing this mode of presentation she would limit access to her film, owing to exhibition technology: "I knew going into it that it would limit the amount of theaters we can play *Meek*'s at. Sadly, very few theaters have the capabilities."[38] However, in the end, *Meek's* release was on a similar scale to that of *Wendy and Lucy*.[39] Reichardt responds to questions about the "kitschy" element of using the old Hollywood aspect ratio by saying: "[W]hen you read back about the period, widescreen was what was kitschy. It was a gimmick! It's what 3D or IMAX is to us today."[40] The choice of screen ratio did make a difference for radio personality Terry Gross: she felt that something seemed wrong with the film, and wanted to pull back the curtain on either side of the screen. In a more serious vein, Gross articulates that the bonnets and the square frame contributed to her "claustrophobia in a wide open space," as the former might have done for the pioneer women, mirroring their social constriction as women.[41] *Meek's Cutoff* succeeds in its depiction of a difficult, alienating, and dangerous journey for the women, but this aesthetic of authenticity made it risky for the actors, as Reichardt attests: "the combination of the oxen and the bonnets . . . take away any peripheral vision. So if oxen have gone nuts next to one of the actresses, they can't necessarily tell."[42] Working with period dress and transportation, Reichardt and her crew must have gained a deeper level of respect and understanding for the effort and ingenuity required by the pioneers to complete a westward journey. Another inspiration for the square framing was found in Robert Adams's contemporary western photography. Reichardt wanted to achieve a "practical and aesthetic" effect: "The square . . . changes the landscape completely—enabling you to get the height over the mountain range and the foreground of the desert—and changes time. It keeps you in the present, where the characters are. I had a rule that there would be no vistas, because I didn't want to be romanticizing the West."[43] Reichardt's desire to adjust her audience's expectations through narrowing the frame and avoiding quick action in an effort to stay in the present locates her aesthetic within the slow cinematic tradition.

SLOW CINEMA AND NEO-NEOREALISM

In a 2010 *Sight and Sound* article, "In Search of Lost Time," Jonathan Romney elaborates on the ability of slow cinema to address politics and culture by slowing down action and creating gaps: "But while certain films reward us with an exalted reverie, certainly of value in itself, slow cinema's capacity to suspend our impulses and reactions can also help us to engage more reflexively with the world in a way that can be critical and indeed political."[44] By extending the length of each shot and compressing the visual elements via the square format, Reichardt creates a space for audience participation. This thought-filled engagement is championed by *New York Times* critic Manohla Dargis, who in her co-authored article "In Defense of the Slow and the Boring" reassures viewers: "Faced with duration not distraction, your mind may wander, but there's no need for panic: it will come back. In wandering there can be revelation."[45] In an industry that has the power to hold spectators' attention and dictate narrative, providing this space for reflection can be interpreted as a subversive act. The exposition scenes in *Meek's Cutoff* exemplify the characteristics of slow cinema. The film begins with a three-minute and 38-second segment with no dialogue. The intertitle orients spectators by stating that the setting is Oregon, 1845; then, to the sound of rushing water, a man leads a team of oxen followed by a covered wagon through a deepening river. The camera follows the team until the very last piece of wagon can be seen, and then cuts to the second location to show a family very slowly unloading a wagon to carry items across the river. No character speaks until seven minutes into the film; this silence enables viewers to absorb the visual components of the situation. When a film opens in such a manner, it resists what David Bordwell calls "intensified continuity" editing, which has taken over mainstream Hollywood film—for example, *The Bourne Ultimatum* (Paul Greengrass, 2007) generates a shot length of just under two seconds.[46] Because slow cinema resists Hollywood-style temporal editing, critics have characterized it as "a form of cultural resistance."[47] In "Towards an Aesthetic of Slow in Contemporary Cinema," Matthew Flanagan suggests that intensified continuity "has transformed a cinema of efficacy into a cinema of acceleration, giving way to a dominant practice" which creates "perpetual, perspectiveless flux, a flux which defers judgment to a later, saner time, which never comes."[48] By rejecting the Western genre label and incorporating slow cinema, *Meek's Cutoff* is in direct opposition to this "cinema of acceleration." Since Reichardt shows action in real time, she creates empathy that, it could be argued, is hard to achieve with intensified continuity editing. Slow cinema may be helping audiences to find and solidify otherwise fleeting empathic threads so that they experience greater understanding, which may in turn act as a means of reflection.

Reichardt is working with what Flanagan labels the "aesthetic of slow" and in doing so, engaging the subversive qualities of slow cinema. While slow cinema is a trend that is cropping up throughout contemporary filmmaking, pinning it down takes research and multiple sources. Jonathan Romney defines slow cinema as "slow, poetic, contemplative—cinema that downplays event in [favor] of mood, evocativeness and an intensified sense of temporality. Such films highlight the viewing process itself as a real-time experience."[49] In addition to Romney's definition, other criteria include the use of ambiguity and openness as a way of encouraging audience reflection and contemplation. But critics of slow cinema point out other, less flattering characteristics such as "ultra-long takes, slender or non-existent narrative, and what they regard as its indifference or even hostility to audiences."[50] In his article "Slow Cinema Backlash" for IFC, Vadim Rizov says, "The problem isn't the masters. It's the second-tier wave of films that premiere at Berlin and smaller festivals . . . and simply stagnate in their own self-righteous slowness . . . those that do [see them] instantly understand why someone would wish a pox upon the whole movement."[51] Rizov closes with this startling and over-generalized statement, leaving the distinction between "masters" and "second-tier" filmmakers open. This oversimplification of "slow" aesthetics by many critics overlooks a connection between slow cinema and André Bazin's concept of "total cinema," which posits that early filmmakers "saw the cinema as a total and complete representation of reality; they saw [. . .] the reconstruction of a perfect illusion of the outside world in sound, color, and relief."[52] In addition to deeper contemplation, mixing slow cinema with experimental elements is a powerful tool for examining classical Western conventions in relation to realism. While Bazin is discussing technical innovations that move cinema closer to the ability to replicate reality, he also refers to an "integral realism" that creates "an image unburdened by the freedom of interpretation of the artist or the irreversibility of time"—which can easily be seen in slow cinema's intentionally open or ambiguous images and gaps.[53] Working within Bazin's theoretical framework, filmmakers like Reichardt, who practice slow cinema and whose goals match, whether intentionally or not, those of "total cinema's" effort to replicate reality, fit into a larger cinematic tradition; slow cinema then begins to complicate larger questions and debates around crafting film.

In his article "Beyond Neo-Neo Realism," James Lattimer reconceptualises the link between Bazin and Reichardt by arguing that Reichardt's style at first seems to epitomize Bazin's "episodic mode" narrative requirements by using real time to create a "cinema of duration" and giving everyday occurrences narrative weight equal to that of heightened action scenes.[54] Lattimer suggests, however, that Reichardt complicates Bazin's requirements through her emphasis on unusual events. One such scene is the initial surprise meeting of Emily and the Cayuse. After the men have left camp and Emily is gathering firewood,

Figure 7.1 Emily shooting and reloading the rifle

she bends to pick up a stick and audiences see the Cayuse's moccasin-covered foot at the same moment she does. Emily freezes and drops the wood, and the two characters run from each other, he toward his horse and she for a rifle. Viewers watch Emily run almost all the way to her wagon, pull the gun out and begin to load it painstakingly, then shoot once, clean it and reload to finally deliver the second warning shot. Because audiences witness the time it takes to retrieve, load, shoot, clean, and reload a rifle, they experience the intensity of the pioneers' growing fear in the dawning knowledge that no one is close enough to come to their aid (Figure 7.1). There are no shot/reverse shots, time lapses, musical cues, or any action at all that would indicate a resolution. In other words, audiences see Emily's action in real time and it "carries [equal] weight," but Reichardt goes further and "gives [the scene and others like it] the kind of additional weight that Bazin's episodic model is concerned with avoiding."[55] Instead of highlighting only realistic moments, as Bazin discusses, Reichardt creates "a new strategy . . . that aims to accentuate the narrative's dramatic construction rather than allowing it to disappear into realist transparency."[56] By doing this, Reichardt keeps spectators aware of the film narrative instead of being lost in the representation of reality, and this exposes the influence of her earlier, more experimental style, found in *River of Grass*. Showing "central dramatic episodes in real time" is the opposite of Bazin's "episodic mode," which calls for a focus on everyday action; but as Lattimer suggests, many of the seemingly non-daily actions were in reality everyday actions for a pioneer working to settle in the American West. Lattimer concludes that Reichardt is "retooling" neorealism and this, in conjunction with her slow cinematic techniques, allows her audience time to grasp her political layerings. These scenes reveal Reichardt's political and social commentary, serving to uncover or "rediscover" the female pioneers' struggle. In addition, they draw our attention to the usual "ellipsis" in the classical Hollywood Western by submerging audiences in the rarely articulated female experience of settling the West.

Reichardt's decisions to align slow cinematic pacing with neo-neorealism and to focus on gendered expectations and experiences via our protagonist, Emily, constitute a unique and effective combination that conveys the difficult physical and emotional environment endured by pioneer women on the Oregon Trail. Attention to everyday detail in a form whose basis is akin to documentary, considering Reichardt's use of historical journals, allows spectators to assume the pioneer women's limited physical vision, mirrored by the aspect ratio:

> In reading the diaries, I got a different picture [to the one] captured in Westerns, which are made up of masculine moments of conflict and conquering. You see that the women are in a similar situation as the Indian or the little boy. Basically, if you're not a white man, you're outside the decision-making process.[57]

This state of affairs is reiterated each time the pioneer women are cut out of a critical navigation meeting. However, by unpacking the layers of the women's mundane acts, Reichardt inserts political commentary and creates a film that engages audiences in a visual conversation about female leadership, drive, determination, and perseverance, as well as their social limitations and expectations. While history books acknowledge male accomplishments and record extraordinary heroic feats of men's survival, there is traditionally very little said about pioneer women's bravery and even less discussion of their everyday tasks. In a three-minute, twenty-two-second scene, Reichardt illustrates the morning responsibilities of pioneer women travelling west. Using only available light, the scene opens with a shot of the early morning sky and then cuts to Emily, who lights a lantern and begins to comb out her hair, the first step in her routine; the next scene is a forty-three-second wide-angle shot that shows her lighting a campfire as two identical fires are started behind her by Glory and Millie. As viewers watch in real time, Emily pours water into a coffee tin and then slowly grinds coffee beans. The camera creates a pattern of abrupt cuts that linger long enough to keep spectators off balance. Operating with little to no light was challenging for Reichardt's crew, but she wanted to depict realistic conditions for pioneer women: "I wanted it to appear to be all lanterns and firelight, to get the sense of how dark it was while, in some scenes, being able to see the whole camp set up—the wagons, the tents, actors coming and going through the camp. Chris [Blauvelt, the cinematographer] was able to achieve that using fires and candles and a really minimal lighting kit."[58] Not only do these shots illustrate with little to no dialogue how difficult life was for pioneers, they also show the expectations placed on women: they are expected to march all day with little to no say about the direction chosen, but they wake before the others in camp to provide meals. Romney comments on the ability of slow cinema to address politics and culture through slowing down action and creating gaps: "But while certain films reward us with an exalted reverie, certainly of value in itself, Slow Cinema's capacity to suspend our impulses and reactions can also help us to engage more reflexively with the world in a way that can be critical and indeed political."[59] By extending the length of each shot and engaging the audience's attention, Reichardt creates a space for additional narrative controlled by the audience. In an industry that has the power to hold spectators' attention and dictate narrative, providing this space can be interpreted by some as a subversive act. It is the denial of action in these experientially credible and slow scenes that speaks to Reichardt's political and social commentary on gender.

"POLITICKING," RACE, AND VIOLENCE

Gender politics are not the only ideological domain with which *Meek's Cutoff* engages; Reichardt and Jon Raymond also reference broader historical and contemporary geopolitical values. Western expansion invites discussion about manifest destiny, a contested ideology even at its height in the mid nineteenth century.[60] Reichardt only hints at Meek's views concerning manifest destiny, a Providential decree to settle the western frontier spreading "republican democracy" at all costs; but during 1845 to 1846, a political battle raged over which nation—Britain or America—would control the Oregon territory.[61] Immigrants were caught in the middle, as the film illustrates through multiple hushed conversations and one campfire debate in which Millie Gately (Zoe Kazan), seemingly speaking for everyone except Meek, hopes "the territory will go American." This political sentiment is what endangers them, if their fears that Meek has led them astray simply to keep immigrants out of the territory prove founded. Reichardt manages to encapsulate historical bias and political debate, projecting these fears onto contemporary issues concerning immigration reform, faulty leadership, and racial prejudice. By the same token, *Meek's Cutoff* is full of social, ethnic, and racial "others," considering that the pioneers are immigrants trying to settle on land that does not belong to them. Their conversations reflect the historical tensions of the period, in particular when Solomon calms fears that Meek is really driving them on a death march. As the audience strains to hear the men's conversation, they are allowed only as much information as Emily and Glory, so it is through a female perspective that viewers hear the first snatches of this news. Later, Solomon tells Emily what was said: "Thomas argued that Meek has taken us off track on purpose; he was hired to get rid of American immigrants. The more of us that come, the more likely the territory will go American—it has a logic." This internal fear gives way to the perceived external threat by the Cayuse tribesman and his search party, so that the film begins to focus on racial bias and stereotypes. A hierarchy has clearly been established even before the capture of the Native American, as indicated by the multiple white male conclaves; but Reichardt continually subverts this by keeping Emily the focus of the film and having her slowly take leadership, in addition to defending their captive. At the risk of spectator alienation, the Cayuse tribesman never speaks English: he communicates through the Nez Perce tribal language, facial expressions, and gestures. Reichardt and Raymond shared a concern that viewers might not connect to his character.[62] Raymond has talked about their decision, saying:

> It was something we were very conscientious of. For myself, the movie ends up being in many ways about racism and racist projections on kind of a cipher. It's a fine line . . . how to create a kind of screen for those kind of projections without also dehumanizing a person. I think it's really important that the audience not understand what he was saying . . . keeping the audience in that position of not knowing was really one of the goals, and the whole ending really depends on just not knowing about his intentions.[63]

An event that turns the tide for the captive is his show of concern and assistance when William, Glory's husband, succumbs to dehydration. In a wide long shot of the entire caravan, William falls and immediately the women run to his aid. Glory stops the oxen, and the next shot is of her cradling her husband's head in her lap, softly explaining that he has refused to drink water all day. The scene is framed by the concerned pioneers huddling closely around William and his wife as Emily retrieves a cooking pot of water, showing the futility of any medical care they can provide. Viewers quickly realize how isolated they are, and how ineffectual their medical methods. As the camera pans for a close-up of Jimmy's face, behind him the Cayuse tribesman walks up, begins singing, and sprinkles dust near William's head. It is clear to viewers and the stunned pioneers that William is receiving a Native American healing ceremony, and that the concern for life is not simply a white man's preoccupation. The camera takes its time panning from character to character and when it cuts to Meek, viewers interpret slight shame in his downcast eyes. The next shot shows a threesome: Millie's tear-streaked and disbelieving face, Solomon's gentle shock, and, after a full gaze at the singing and dancing

Cayuse, Thomas looking shamefully down and adjusting his hat. The camera lingers on Glory's resigned face and freely flowing tears, and when she looks down, not bothering to wipe them away, viewers see Emily turning to stare at the Cayuse as he finishes and walks away. While spectators only see the back of her bonneted head and a bit of her profile, they register her new sense of faith in their Native American guide.

The Cayuse's prayer for William's health is not the first time religion is inserted into the film. Religious sentiments are sprinkled throughout thanks to the White family, and the representation of spirituality from the Cayuse might be what helps shame the pioneers during the prayer dance scene. Meek uses religion as a means to justify his racism and his continued call for hanging or shooting the Cayuse captive. Words familiar to the Western genre like "savage" and "heathen" come to Meek's aid in convincing the group that during a Native American attack everyone is slaughtered, including women and children. Meek's resistance to their captive's spirituality, which helps to humanize him, suggests modern extreme right-wing Christian ideology, since it was historically the early roots of Christian practice during the settlement of the West. The choice to give the most religious of the pioneer families the surname White could be an indication of this ideological link between Christianity and racist or intolerant practices. Even as the ending is informed by the Cayuse prayer song and dance scene, however, audiences can only guess whether the Cayuse is truly leading them to salvation.

Many analogies have been drawn between the George W. Bush administration's second term and Meek's consistent reassurances that the group is "not lost, [we] are just finding our way." Both Raymond and Reichardt felt the storyline lent itself to a comment on issues of race and oppression since the opening of the Guantanamo Bay prison and the ensuing suspicion that the US was condoning torture:

> When we were working on the script it was the time of Guantanamo
> . . . Certainly what was appealing about Meek's story was that it felt
> as though there were a lot of contemporary themes in it. We had to
> back away from that and get into the pioneers' story, but throughout
> the making of the film, and as I was cutting, the political landscape
> changed. I found that whatever was happening in the news daily was so
> easy to project on to what I was working with . . . American history is so
> repetitive . . . [since often it highlights] issues of conquest and whose life
> has more value—which comes down to racism. [64]

It is not difficult to believe that the abuse endured by the Cayuse captive—a kick to the head when Meek is questioning him, and the withholding of food and water—allude to the Bush administration's interrogations of terror suspects: "Meek increasingly becomes a Rorschach test, resembling a number of leaders, elected and otherwise, we might all know."[65] After the Tetherow wagon crashes in a ravine, and Meek threatens to kill the Cayuse for not obeying his command to drop the sewing basket Emily used to repair his shoe, the violence seems reminiscent of the waterboarding torture scenes in Kathryn Bigelow's *Zero Dark Thirty* (2012). The films are linked by the Bush era's war tactics and the use of fear and torture to coerce captives. In multiple scenes, Reichardt's film asks the question, "Can nations expand without violence— and violent men?"[66] In one interview, moreover, she refers to historical evidence about Meek's incompetent character and then makes an unguarded joke labelling Bush and Meek as unsuccessful leaders: "Meek was perceived in different ways by different people, but definitely was thought of as someone who didn't know what he was doing by pretty much everyone"—which, she explains, is supported in his fourteen-page autobiography, where he illustrates his incompetency. "Ten pages is this long-winded joke, and then he's just like, 'I led the first wagon train through Oregon territory. Completely successful.' Probably just like George W. Bush's new book: 'Everything went great. Not to worry.'"[67] Elsewhere, though, Reichardt tends to play down direct connections to any political administration, saying the film revolves around the question of leadership and community decisions:

> [It is] this idea of a persuasive blowhard persuading a bunch of people out into the middle of the desert without really knowing the lay of the land or possibly being without any kind of real plan and just overestimating himself and this situation and then winding up at the mercy of people that he is culturally completely different than and is mistrustful of . . . it has all these contemporary components to it.[68]

Emily might represent a new administration with a more humane answer to violent interrogation methods when she pulls her gun on Meek and says, "I'd be wary." Though her regime is more progressive, Emily's empathy is tempered by her ambivalence, racism, and desire for the Cayuse to "owe her something." While Emily's confrontation with Meek involves few words, the scene is powerful; Emily assumes true ownership of the caravan, but at a price, since she has to "act like a man—by threatening to shoot Meek."[69] The pioneers' misguided trust in Meek did not ultimately turn deadly for many who followed him in 1845, but it does serve as a cautionary tale for contemporary times.

As seen in the standoff between Emily and Meek, the threat of violence is ever-present on the screen. Reichardt builds suspense, keeping the tension bubbling just under the surface, ready to explode at any point as the narrative progresses. Spectators brace themselves for an angry revolt against Meek, a racially motivated attack by Meek upon their Native American captive, or the slaughter of the caravan by a Cayuse slave-trading party. Millie is a big part of the anxiety as she progressively spirals downward into the delirium of terror, most notably after finding a chalk symbol written on a rock by the Cayuse captive, and then again after finding a symbolic lone tree in the desert. In her high-pitched whine she pleads to her husband to turn back, that "we still have time." This comes after her earlier chants of "They're coming; they're coming," referring to the possibility of a Cayuse search party. Millie's reactions remind spectators of the caravan's precarious situation. Besides Millie's dialogue, Reichardt conveys the deepening sense of fear through body language and sound on the final day of their journey. Beginning with a high angle shot from the top of the cliffs the group is walking beside, white chalk symbols are shown covering the cliffs, leaving the pioneers and the audience nervous and fearful. Reichardt uses Millie's body and mannerisms as an unnerving symbol of their destitution. The eerie cello music begins softly, almost unnoticeable—until the camera falls on Millie and the volume rises sharply, reminding viewers that any member of the group could begin spiraling into her terrorized state of mind. While each character is observed by the camera as they walk by the marked rock walls, Millie is undoubtedly the focal point as she stumbles along, arms bent and away from her body, at times childlike in her attempts to reach toward her husband, who avoids all contact with her. Meek, on his horse with gun cocked, mumbles to himself and, in a close-up, laughs as if contemplating the group's violent murder at the hands of the Cayuse. Solomon and the White family, in separate cameos, turn their heads as if hearing something offscreen, and even the robust and reassuring Emily looks grave. The fear of violence is accentuated in this scene through body language, close-ups, and music, and the audience's endurance is rewarded by a nerve-splitting finale as the scene smash-cuts to complete silence and a still, flat landscape.

Reichardt has offered a revolutionized feminist Western by using a female protagonist who assumes leadership, and historical documents to create a realistic experience of 1845; but she also changes the conventions of genre by using real-time pacing for the dialogue and action of the film:

Nothing is quick. In Westerns, everything is quick and highlighted. So we really wanted to play with that . . . I'm taken aback by the comment that it's slow, but then I guess if I go to a new film and sit through the trailers, I feel a little bombarded by the instant everything . . . our sense of time has changed so dramatically. Our expectations about time in cinema in the U.S., I don't know where it goes from here.[70]

Hollywood viewers are trained to expect fast-paced narratives, and *Meek's Cutoff* offers the opposite, but mixing "slow cinema" with alternatives to traditional genres can be a very powerful and liberating tool.

THE OPEN IMAGE IN SLOW CINEMA

As well as spirituality,[71] a core attribute of slow cinema is its ambiguity and openness. By its very nature, slow cinema invites viewer input and spectator ownership with its gaps and pauses. In their article "The Open Image: Poetic Realism and the New Iranian Cinema," Shohini Chaudhuri and Howard Finn suggest that through the use of the open image Iranian cinema allows spectators to realize multiple truths: "The open images of Iranian film remind us of the loss of such images in most contemporary cinema, the loss of cinema's particular space for creative interpretation and critical reflection."[72] While Chaudhuri and Finn make a convincing case that the open image is pervasive in Iranian cinema, it is not exclusive to new Iranian cinema. The neorealist settings of American indie films like *Meek's Cutoff* allow for what Chaudhuri and Finn characterize as an "aesthetic of stasis" that can be traced to Italian neorealism.[73] They cite the freeze-frame ending of François Truffaut's *400 Blows* and suggest that just like the open image, these freeze-frame images not only defer the ending but when the image is in stasis or "'stops, the viewer keeps going, moving deeper and deeper, one might say, into the image.'"[74] A merging of image and spectator for prolonged meditation is one of the desired outcomes for slow cinema audiences, and the open image is the perfect vehicle.

Chaudhuri and Finn's discussion of "obsessive framing" (from Pier Paolo Pasolini's essay "The Cinema of Poetry") as a characteristic of the open image is applicable when focusing on Reichardt's decision to shoot her film in 1:37:1 ratio. As many Iranian filmmakers (such as those trained in the House of Makhmalbaf or Abbas Kiarostami) frame their scenes with doorways or "close-ups of disembodied women's hands," Reichardt pushes this concept and frames every scene so that neither the pioneers nor viewers "see what tomorrow is and what yesterday was" as they march through the desert."[75] In addition to the ratio framing, the women's bonnets and the covered wagons function much like the Iranian doorways by creating an "internal frame, marking the barrier to our vision, and emphasizing the selectiveness of what we see," which helps create tension and empathy for the characters in addition to propelling the aesthetic.[76] No matter the method or type, any open image in slow cinema is meant to create thought and contemplation.

Reichardt also makes use of the open image in a sequence in which Emily tries to lighten the load in the wagon by throwing out possessions. The camera moves into the covered wagon as Emily picks up a rocking chair and, after

Figure 7.2 The caravan finds a lone tree

some effort, hoists it out the back opening. The camera stays stationary and after a moment the chair, seat facing down, comes into focus and is centered within the arch of the wagon "bonnet" covering. The covering reminds spectators of other point of view shots that are framed by the women's bonnets. This "obsessive framing" of the chair becomes the open image, and it stays centered within the wagon bonnet frame. The chair's meaning is open because it represents more than just a practical plan for survival. It might represent the lack of respect for the land and culture of Native Americans by settlers, or it could be symbolic of the displacement of the domestic and "feminine" comforts in a harsh reality; but no matter the meaning, situating the chair as an open image contributes to spectator ownership and input.

Reichardt closes her film with a specific type of open image, the "crystal image," or as Chaudhuri and Finn describe it, one that "is too ambiguous, too 'strong,' to be reduced to one level of interpretation."[77] This ambiguity allows audiences to create space for reflection and inner debate. At the end of the film, the caravan finds a lone tree in the desert (Figure 7.2). A stationary camera centers the tree in the frame as the community, one by one, rush toward it. The tree suggests a close water source, but once again, the issue of trust crops up. After the group confirms their agreement to follow their Cayuse guide, Emily looks through two intertwined branches and the camera does a shot/reverse shot sequence framing her worried, soot-streaked and intent face between the branches. Spectators see, with the reverse shot, Emily looking at their Native American guide as she contemplates their decision to trust and

Figure 7.3 Emily, framed by the lone tree, looks at the Native American guide

Figure 7.4 The Native American guide stares at Emily framed by the tree

follow him (Figure 7.3). He returns her gaze and then turns and slowly walks away from the group, framed between the same branches. As the screen fades to black, viewers are left creating multiple narratives and possibilities for the survival story of Emily's lost pioneer caravan (Figure 7.4).

Meek's Cutoff offers spectators, then, a historically researched, authentic-feeling and politically charged atypical Western through its use of slow cinematic qualities, neo-neorealism and open-ended narrative structures eschewing gun battles, fast-paced action, and other expected genre conventions. Slow cinema shows the everyday in real time, revives a spiritual component through art, and forms open images through stasis, but its contribution to the deceleration of our culture may be its most important legacy. With the help of slow cinematic qualities Reichardt deconstructs the classical Hollywood Western, so the focus is on pioneer women and their experience of settling in the American West. The title *Meek's Cutoff* alludes to the termination of Meek's faulty leadership at the hands of women—so it is fitting that a woman filmmaker, whose stories are often also "lost" in Hollywood, has rediscovered the stories of women pioneers. Through her form and content Reichardt exploits genre conventions more often than not to subversive ends, making visible those who have been written out of patriarchal histories.

NOTES

E. Dawn Hall, "Gender Politics in Kelly Reichardt's Feminist Western *Meek's Cutoff*," in Katarzyna Paszkiewicz and Mary Harrod (eds.), *Women's Authorship and Genre in Film* (Abingdon: Routledge, forthcoming).

1. Sam Adams, "Kelly Reichardt and Jon Raymond," The A.V. Club, 26 April 2011, <https://film.avclub.com/kelly-reichardt-and-jon-raymond-1798225326> (accessed 20 September 2017); James Ponsoldt, "Lost in America: Kelly Reichardt's 'Meek's Cutoff,'" *Filmmaker Magazine*, November 2011, <http://filmmakermagazine.com/35034-lost-in-america-kelly-reichardts-meeks-cutoff/#.WGQDIlMrJow> (accessed 20 September 2017).
2. Adams, "Kelly Reichardt and Jon Raymond."
3. Ibid.
4. Graham Fuller, "The Oregon Trail," *Sight & Sound* 21, no. 5 (2011): 41.
5. Ibid.
6. Ibid. pp. 41–2.
7. Adams, "Kelly Reichardt and Jon Raymond."
8. Ryan Gilbey, "Kelly Reichardt: How I Trekked Across Oregon for *Meek's Cutoff* Then Returned to Teaching," *The Guardian*, 8 April 2011, <https://www.theguardian.com/film/2011/apr/09/kelly-reichardt-meeks-cutoff> (accessed 20 September 2017).
9. "*Meek's Cutoff*," *Box Office Mojo*, <http://www.boxofficemojo.com/movies/?id=meekscutoff.htm> (accessed 20 September 2017).
10. Ibid.
11. Ibid.
12. Reichardt quoted in Gilbey, "Kelly Reichardt."
13. Reichardt quoted in Ponsoldt, "Lost in America."
14. "About Us," *Cinetic Media*, <https://www.cineticmedia.com/about-us> (accessed 20 September 2017).
15. "*Meek's Cutoff* (2010): Awards," *Internet Movie Database*, <http://www.imdb.com/title/tt1518812/awards?ref_=tt_awd> (accessed 20 September 2017).

16. Reichardt quoted in Ponsoldt, "Lost in America."
17. Ibid.
18. Reichardt quoted in Stephen Saito, "Kelly Reichardt on Surviving 'Meek's Cutoff,'" *IFC*, 22 April 2011, <http://www.ifc.com/2011/04/kelly-reichardt-meeks-cutoff> (accessed 20 September 2017).
19. Reichardt quoted in Karina Longworth, "Kelly Reichardt Explains 'Meek's Cutoff,' Her Latest Road Movie," *San Francisco Weekly*, 4 May 2011, <https://archives.sfweekly. com/sanfrancisco/kelly-reichardt-explains-meeks-cutoff-her-latest-road-movie/ Content?oid=2181363> (accessed 20 September 2017).
20. Reichardt quoted in Ponsoldt, "Lost in America."
21. Ibid.
22. Ibid.
23. Reichardt quoted in Gilbey, "Kelly Reichardt."; Fuller, "The Oregon Trail," p. 42.
24. Reichardt quoted in Ponsoldt, "Lost in America."
25. Michelle Williams interviewed by S. T. Vanairsdale, "Michelle Williams on Meek's Cutoff, Goodbyes and Getting Lost at the Movies," *MovieLine*, 30 March 2011, <http:// movieline.com/2011/03/30/michelle-williams-on-meeks-cutoff-goodbyes-and-getting-lost-at-the-movies/> (accessed 20 September 2017).
26. Adams, "Kelly Reichardt and Jon Raymond."
27. Jamie Dunn, "Kelly Reichardt: Redefining the Western," *The Skinny*, 7 April 2011, <http://www.theskinny.co.uk/film/interviews/kelly-reichardt-redefining-the-western> (accessed 20 September 2017).
28. "Going West: The Making Of 'Meek's Cutoff,'" *Fresh Air*, National Public Radio (WHYY, Philadelphia), 4 April 2011, <http://www.npr.org/2011/04/14/135206694/ going-west-the-making-of-meeks-cutoff> (accessed 20 September 2017).
29. Rick Altman, *Film/Genre* (London: BFI, 1999), p. 70, p. 82.
30. Ibid. p. 35.
31. Ibid. p. 41.
32. Ibid. p. 40.
33. Ibid. p. 218.
34. Reichardt quoted in "Going West."
35. Mark Adams, "Meek's Cutoff," *Screendaily*, 6 September 2010, <http://www. screendaily.com/reviews /latest-reviews/-meeks-cutoff/5017812.article#> (accessed 20 September 2017).
36. Reichardt quoted in Anne Thompson, "Meek's Cutoff: Professor Kelly Reichardt's Filmmaking 101 Primer," *IndieWire*, 21 April 2011.
37. Reichardt quoted in Fuller, "The Oregon Trail," p. 41.
38. Reichardt quoted in Jesse Hawthorne Ficks, "Northwest Passage: Kelly Reichardt on 'Meek's Cutoff,'" *San Francisco Bay Guardian Online*, 3 May 2011, <http://48hills.org/ sfbgarchive/2011/05/03/northwest-passage-kelly-reichardt-meeks-cutoff/> (accessed 20 September 2017).
39. Ibid.; *"Meek's Cutoff," Box Office Mojo*.
40. Reichardt quoted in Ficks, "Northwest Passage."
41. Reichardt quoted in "Going West."
42. Reichardt quoted in Ponsoldt, "Lost in America."
43. Reichardt quoted in Fuller, "The Oregon Trail," p. 42.
44. Jonathan Romney, "In Search of Lost Time," *Sight and Sound* 20, no. 2 (2010): 43–4.
45. Manohla Dargis and A. O. Scott, "In Defense of the Slow and the Boring," *The*

New York Times, 3 June 2011: 10, <http://www.nytimes.com/2011/06/05/movies/ films-in-defense-of-slow-and-boring.html> (accessed 20 September 2017).

46. Matthew Flanagan, "Towards an Aesthetic of Slow in Contemporary Cinema," *16:9 Film Journal* 6, no. 29 (2008), <http://www.16-9.dk/2008-11/side11_inenglish.htm> (accessed 20 September 2017).

47. Sukhdev Sandhu, "'Slow Cinema' Fights Back against Bourne's Supremacy," *The Guardian*, 9 March 2012, <https://www.theguardian.com/film/2012/mar/09/slow-cinema-fights-bournes-supremacy> (accessed 20 September 2017).

48. Flanagan, "Towards an Aesthetic of Slow."

49. Romney, "In Search of Lost Time."

50. Sandhu, "'Slow Cinema' Fights Back."

51. Vadim Rizov, "Slow Cinema Backlash," <http://www.ifc.com/2010/05/slow-cinema-backlash> (accessed 20 September 2017).

52. André Bazin, "The Myth of Total Cinema," in Leo Braudy and Marshall Cohen (eds.), *Film Theory and Criticism*, 5th edn. (New York: Oxford University Press, 1999), p. 201.

52. Ibid.

53. Ibid. p. 202.

54. James Lattimer, "Beyond Neo-Neo Realism: Reconfigurations of Neorealist Narration in Kelly Reichardt's *Meek's Cutoff*," *Cinephile* 7, no. 2 (2011): 38.

55. Ibid. p. 40.

56. Ibid.

57. Reichardt quoted in Fuller, "The Oregon Trail," p. 41.

58. Reichardt quoted in Ponsoldt, "Lost in America."

59. Romney, "In Search of Lost Time."

60. Trevor B. McCrisken, "Exceptionalism: Manifest Destiny," in *Encyclopedia of American Foreign Policy* (New York: Scribner, 2002), p. 68.

61. Ibid.

62. Adams, "Kelly Reichardt and Jon Raymond."

63. Jon Raymond quoted in Adams, "Kelly Reichardt and Jon Raymond."

64. Reichardt quoted in Fuller, "The Oregon Trail," p. 42.

65. Pondsolt, "Lost in America."

66. Ibid.

67. Longworth, "Kelly Reichardt Explains."

68. Reichardt quoted in Saito, "Kelly Reichardt."

69. Reichardt quoted in Fuller, "The Oregon Trail," p. 41.

70. Reichardt quoted in Adams, "Kelly Reichardt and Jon Raymond."

71. According to Romney, "the current Slow Cinema might be seen as a response to a bruisingly pragmatic decade in which, post-9/11, the oppressive everyday awareness of life as overwhelmingly political, economic and ecological would seem to preclude (in the West, at least) any spiritual dimension in art."

72. Shohini Chaudhuri and Howard Finn, "The Open Image: Poetic Realism and the New Iranian Cinema," in Annette Kuhn and Catherine Grant (eds.), *Screening World Cinema* (New York and London: Routledge, 2006), p. 179.

73. Ibid. p. 165.

74. Paul Schrader, *Transcendental Style in Cinema: Ozu, Bresson, Dreyer* (New York: Da Capo, 1972), p. 161 (quoted in Chaudhuri and Finn, "The Open Image").

75. Reichardt quoted in "Going West."

76. Ibid.

77. Chaudhuri and Finn, "The Open Image," p. 179.

CHAPTER 8

Expansion: *Night Moves*

[O]ptions are laid on the table from different characters . . . all trying to be some kind of pull against the destruction of the planet . . . If this more radical approach is the wrong approach, what is the right one?—Kelly Reichardt[1]

Reichardt's fifth film, *Night Moves* (2013), a political thriller about ecoterrorism, represents an adjustment in form, style, and content compared to her prior body of work. Though on the surface *Night Moves* appears to have more commercial intentions, it might be her most overt challenge to cinematic commercialization. Although its thriller genre promises sex, action, and special effects, the film defies expectations by never showing these events on screen. In present-day Oregon, Josh (Jesse Eisenberg), a worker at an organic farm, connects Dena, a day spa worker (Dakota Fanning) to Harmon, a reclusive ex-marine (Peter Sarsgaard), and together they blow up a local dam, hoping that "people are going to start thinking" about wasting natural resources. Dena contributes the funds for the operation, and Harmon agrees to set up the explosives. Especially topical for a contemporary society reeling from terrorist incidents, *Night Moves* examines perpetrator motivation and character breakdown in their aftermath. It invites ethical questions relating to the ecoterrorism of the protagonists and the gender commentary supplied by its sparse dialogue and character interactions.

PRODUCTION

Night Moves premiered at the Venice International Film Festival with a nomination for the Golden Lion award, and almost simultaneously screened at the Toronto International Film Festival (TIFF) and Deauville American Film Festival, winning the Grand Prix at the latter.[2] Distribution was secured at TIFF by Cinedigm Entertainment and is listed, to date, as the second most profitable decision for the company, with a gross total domestically of \$271,755.[3] While the film's widest domestic release was in fifty-six theatres—more than Reichardt's earlier films—it had a shorter life than *Meek's Cutoff* at seventeen weeks, and it made less money (a total of just over \$850,000).[4] While moviegoers in the UK came out in droves to see Shirley Henderson in *Meek's Cutoff*, it was French cinephiles who most heavily patronized *Night Moves*, unsurprising since it received the Grand Prix award at Deauville.

Reichardt, as usual, retained a number of crew members from her earlier films. Familiar faces such as Neil Kopp and Anish Savjani (Filmscience), who both produced Reichardt's last four films, and Christopher Blauvelt, director of photography on *Meek's Cutoff* and *Certain Women* (2016), all worked on *Night Moves*. Reichardt discussed her production methods with Eugene Hernandez in a Film Society of Lincoln Center interview, stating that the shoot lasted just over twenty-two days and took over a year to plan, with three scouting trips.[5] She again teamed up with Jon Raymond to write the screenplay after the storyline germinated following visits to local organic farmers' market communities in southern Oregon.[6] Raymond's desire to explore local politics and Reichardt's interest in both farming and examining processes motivated them to place the film within the heist genre.[7] The two main filming locations—the organic farm that employs Josh, and the dam on the Santiam River—offered challenges on different levels. After scouting over a dozen dams, Neil Kopp worked over the course of a year to gain permission for filming.[8] Reichardt had selected the organic farm early in the process, visiting it and planning all her shots a year prior to shooting, but she had to rethink them due to crop rotations; not only that, but Jesse Eisenberg, who prepared for his part by living and working on the farm, ended up helping to build a greenhouse in the middle of a field where she had intended to shoot.[9] While Reichardt initially anticipated that shooting boat to boat would be the hardest part of production, she later admitted it was the indoor scenes that caused her the most frustration: "I'm so used to shooting outside. I really found the hardest days was . . . shooting with four walls. I really felt limited. I really need to conquer walls. Interiors are hard for me because I've spent a lot of time shooting outside."[10] Reichardt's distinctive cinematic look, like that of many auteurs, has been shaped by her method of production. Years of shooting on location with natural light and source sound mean that this approach is now embedded in her art and process.

Much like Michelle Williams during her time working on *Wendy and Lucy*, Eisenberg, Fanning, and Sarsgaard found that owing to the isolated locations they were unhindered by press or celebrity-seekers. Reichardt explained that cast and crew were treated equally: "It's not just finding the people who are right for the part, it's like trying to anticipate who's going to really be up for what we will put them through."[11] As is the case with many independent, low-budget films, actors and crew worked together to complete filming in the allotted time. While such an approach might be foreign to mainstream stars (Fanning said *Night Moves* was her first experience with this method), it can build intimacy and commitment to the project.[12] Each actor learned about their character differently: Eisenberg asked questions and lived on the farm, Fanning was very private and ignored the box of research Reichardt mailed to her, and Sarsgaard was driving the *Night Moves* boat ten minutes after arriving on set, with no prior face-to-face meetings.[13]

In keeping with Reichardt's other productions, budget concerns drove many of the creative choices on *Night Moves*. Reichardt opted for the first time not to use film, and instead used an ARRI Alexia camera to shoot digitally. She explained that the budget could not support 35mm, and there was not enough light for 16mm film.[14] While she didn't mind using digital, she explained that there were "several shots that would be better caught on film," and though it wasn't "flat," the shots didn't have "light going through" them.[15] Reichardt edited the film herself (as she has done with all her own work apart from *River of Grass*) because "I can afford me," as she explained to an interviewer, going on to discuss her process: "I'm a big believer in letting my films be bad for a long time and whittling away at it slowly. I don't have much footage so it's not tedious."[16] Of all her films, she has said *Night Moves* was the most plot-driven, and while in the editing room she found that this tied her hands.

> This was the first time the film could only be put together in one way . . . I had to stay the course. It was really fun to have that much of a road to follow. I like ambiguity and that's what I want to make films about— but it can't be a mess—so there is a real frame that you can work in . . . language of the film has to be articulate and then it can be about things that are harder to put your finger on.[17]

The film highlights difficult, "hard to put your finger on" issues such as environmentalism, capitalist greed, and psychological breakdowns. In an effort to make sure her ideas were "getting across" Reichardt asked her usual mentors, Todd Haynes and Larry Fessenden, for notes. She also reached out to Gus Van Sant, who reassured her after an initial viewing that the intentions for the characters were clear.[18]

SOUND

The cinematic soundscape of *Night Moves* enhances the intensity of the characters' emotions and actions throughout the film. Its score was created by
composer Jeff Grace, who also worked on *Meek's Cutoff* and *Certain Women*.
Instead of working with music early on, Reichardt sent Grace specific sounds
she wanted to include in the film, and he developed the intense, meditative but
somewhat sinister theme heard throughout. This recurring theme functions
almost as a character, since it signals audiences to be alert and pay attention to
small details. Viewers hear it mainly in connection with Josh, and its intensity
heightens in the second half of the film as he descends into debilitating paranoia.
One example of the swelling theme is Josh's drive home after spying on Dena,
reminiscent of Alfred Hitchcock's *North by Northwest* (1959): headlights appear
in his rear-view mirror, and he eventually succumbs to his suspicions and pulls
over to allow the car to pass. His paranoia is contagious as viewers, with a nudge
from the soundtrack, also begin to sink into his unstable point of view.

Reichardt has remarked light-heartedly on feeling frustrated by critics'
comments on the quietness of her soundscapes. She very intentionally fills up
her films with specific sounds: "I do so much sound work; I'm always like—
are you really listening? Did you hear that mosquito?"[19] To ears unfamiliar
with independent films, her carefully placed tracks of flies in *Meek's Cutoff* or
distant trains in *Wendy and Lucy* might go unnoticed—or, more likely, seem
like happenstance—but each sound has a purpose in her films. A direct result
of shooting on location and outside is an authentic, naturally occurring sound
track such as the sound of wind chimes outside Harmon's trailer as Josh walks
into the wood, or a loud greenhouse fan whirling until Josh turns it off to hear
a car door slam. But what tends to receive more attention is her use of silence;
and while *Night Moves* has her characteristic sparse dialogue, it does seem
noisier than her earlier work. Instead of frequent patches of silence, Grace's
theme is used in transitional scenes, especially pre-explosion; and there seems
to always be some type of source sound to distract from the absence of dialogue. Each time audiences are allowed into the spa Dena works at, there is
noticeable woodland music playing. Even the power sprayer Josh uses at the
car wash gives way to the beeping of heavy machinery pushing waste in a landfill; and while these are seemingly simple sounds, they overwhelm the senses,
contributing to the suspenseful nature of the film.

DEFYING EXPECTATIONS

In what might be an outright snub of action films, Reichardt delivers an explosion, a sex scene, and an FBI investigation, but in a very nontraditional and

Figure 8.1 Josh, Dena, and Harmon hear the dam explode

subversive way. In the dimly lit escape scenes after they have activated the bomb timer, the trio paddle away from the dam and audiences hear their heavy breathing, the crunching of sticks and gravel, and the tension-filled moment of the truck ignition choking—all in anticipation of seeing water burst through an exploded dam. Instead, viewers only hear the explosion, and the camera stays fixed on the three fleeing the area. The audience strains to see their emotional reaction as they sit in a source-lit truck cab, with only Harmon's nervous giggle acknowledging the explosion in the distance (Figure 8.1). As the realization dawns that they have just committed a felony, Dena, sitting between Josh and Harmon, grows tense, and her face reflects the increasingly serious tone of the group. Not only is a visual of the explosion denied, but viewers see no aftermath of the destruction later in the film. Even the website Josh finds dedicated to a hiker drowned in the flood shows no hint of what has happened near the dam. Similarly, in the scene when Josh arrives at Harmon's trailer after dumping materials and washing his truck, he hears a faint giggle from Dena, which suggests she and Harmon are having sex; but contrary to what might be expected in a more mainstream film, audiences are not granted access to their activities. Josh seems nonchalant about this situation, but questions about his relationships with both his partners go unanswered in the film. From the opening scene, Josh and Dena engage in activities often associated with lovers: they gaze at bodies of water, see films together, and purchase large investments. There is also a suggestion of a more intimate relationship between them later in the film when Surprise, Josh's co-worker, asks him if he has talked with Dena after hearing she has been unwell. However, it is Harmon

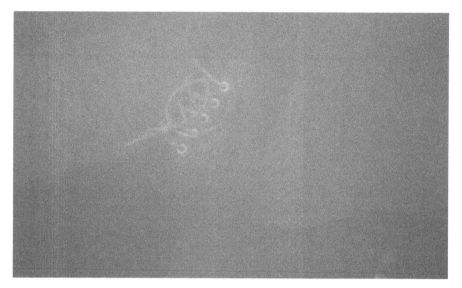

Figure 8.2 Dena's shoe indicates her death

who draws solitary smiles and fleeting laughter from Josh and who is given a goodbye hand-clasp, the only friendly human touch Josh allows in the film. If Josh does feel betrayed, those repressed feelings may help to account for his drunken, paranoid decision to take Dena's life.

Explosions and sex are typically left unexplored in Reichardt's films, but murder seems even more uncharacteristic. Sound and camera angles are crucial in framing the murder scene. As Josh opens the sauna room door, the sizzling of steam is all audiences hear until the low growl Dena utters as she lunges at Josh. The steam is also used to shield her body from viewers, negating voyeurism. While Dena is not given a POV shot in her final moments, the camera focuses mainly on a paranoid and troubled perpetrator, and Dena's shoe movements are the only indication of her death (Figure 8.2). Micro-budget filmmaking calls for creative shots such as these, but they also act to remind viewers of their voyeuristic tendencies and to negate, especially in scenes of sex and murder, an objectifying "male gaze." Josh is motivated to kill Dena because he feels she cannot be trusted, but the murder could also qualify as yet another example of a woman being punished for her sexuality. In her research, Erin Arizzi suggests that Harmon is the real "object of desire" and that Dena's vulnerabilities not only threaten Josh's freedom, but his relationship with Harmon.[20] As the "bond" between the three perpetrators unravels, their personal interconnections take on greater significance than the external investigation. In most films, an active FBI investigation earns more than a few casual mentions and one police checkpoint on the highway; but here, the steady disintegration of the main characters showcases the effects of such an investigation without focusing on police work. Through the paranoia of Josh, Dena, and to a lesser extent Harmon, audiences feel the tension and perceived closeness of the agents. Arizzi aptly sums up the camera's voyeurism by concluding: "The world she reveals in her films is one of constant surveillance, in which both femininity and masculinity have become, for her characters, overwhelming burdens to bear. This is because Reichardt makes films about people living outside of mainstream representations."[21] *Night Moves* mixes road movie with heist genre elements when Josh drives all night and into the morning to escape his crime. Viewers are reminded of Marion Crane's overnight drive in Hitchcock's *PSYCHO* (1960), evoking an inevitable connection between the two films: both Reichardt and Hitchcock highlight surveillance, and the paranoia that contributes to the perception of being watched. However, in *Night Moves* Reichardt is examining more than just the personal domain— she reaches into the public sphere, juxtaposing public safety issues and civil rights/privacy. This is a topic hotly debated in the twenty-first century owing to technological advances and the increase in terrorist acts. Reichardt reminds viewers throughout the film that Josh is highly visible to multiple eyes and cameras—as are members of the audience, once they step out of the theatre.

While *Night Moves* is Reichardt's most plot-driven film to date, with a nod to more commercial characteristics, the tempo of the film still defies a mainstream audiences' expectations. Apart from pockets of tension-filled action scenes, most of the film is a waiting game with the emphasis on extended quiet scenes. Dena's tense search for fertilizer puts viewers on edge, but the scenes that follow focus on processes: mixing the bomb materials, stuffing sandbags full of explosives, ripping out seating in the boat, dumping the leftovers in a landfill, and spraying out any evidence from the truck bed. After the bomb timer is triggered, a car pulls over to change a tire, creating another pocket of tension as the trio debate stopping the countdown; it is then that viewers learn Harmon is unable to disconnect the bomb. Once the car pulls away and the three get to shore, the camera cuts to the canoe floating away from the bank instead of focusing on the characters escaping. When they arrive at Harmon's truck the camera follows Josh slinging his truck hitch into the woods, a seemingly unnecessary detail, before he clasps hands for a quick goodbye with Harmon. In these scenes Reichardt emphasizes process and detail over traditional action, opting to slow down the plot. During the second half of the film, these long takes with little to no dialogue become more prominent as Josh becomes more paranoid. One especially curious scene begins after Josh rushes into the Ashland Public Library to see the tribute website created to honor the hiker who died in the explosion. Josh is staring out from behind a farmers' market booth to see workers reading newspapers, presumably about the explosion, and a police officer looms just outside the market. The officer's presence is another reminder that Josh's actions have brought the entire community

Figure 8.3 Man with a cat in his backpack at the farmers' market

under suspicion. The use of slow motion coupled with Grace's eerie theme music emphasizes his deepening paranoia and unstable mental state. Everyone seems to be staring back at him with disdain, even the somewhat comical dreadlocked man who totes his kitten around in his backpack (Figure 8.3). The ramping effect forces viewers to see from Josh's point of view—and then dumps them back out into reality, as the music abruptly ends and life continues in real time.

While *Night Moves* stands out from her prior films as a plot-driven heist genre drama, Reichardt again uses slow cinematic characteristics to provide meditative moments of reflection and to create tension. *Meek's Cutoff* offered hints of tension-filled meditation, but *Night Moves* fills almost all of its silence and long takes with heightened suspense. Viewers experience prolonged tension in several scenes, such as when Josh and Dena's getaway vehicle rounds the bend after the explosion to see a police roadblock. The female officer slowly checks their truck, and instead of excited chatter or nervous discussion the scene is quiet and uneventful. Later the following day, Josh is working in a greenhouse. The scene creeps along, gradually revealing the level of paranoia that is settling into his consciousness; he is beginning to believe that anyone approaching the farm might be the authorities. Meanwhile, audiences learn how to cut and process acorn squash during the extended scene. Even the scene leading up to Dena's death could be considered slower in pace than a typical action-oriented fight scene. As she closes up the spa after hours, viewers see Dena swing a crystal prism in an attempt to calm her nerves. Unaware that Josh is hiding in a closet watching her, she slowly begins to clean up. When she discovers Josh, the dialogue and action do not speed up; the two of them address each other in broken sentences as she slowly walks toward him. Even after Josh trips Dena and they flounder on the floor, the movement builds anticipation as Josh gathers himself and slowly stands, giving Dena time to escape. Slowing down a murder scene, which is typically quick and action-packed, allows viewers to run different scenarios of the outcome, intensifying the emotional impact. Moreover, slow pacing and the lack of quick cuts add a subversive element by denying viewers what they expect from the heist genre, creating pockets of reflection throughout the film.

POLITICAL CONNECTIONS

While the pacing of the film has its own political intentions, its content can also be linked to contemporary politics. The Occupy Wall Street movement, a protest movement demanding social and economic equality, was most active in America from 2011 to 2012.[22] The movement pushes against the status quo, and consequently capitalism and its effect on the environment is often a topic. In fact, some argue for a "Green Panther Party" patterned after the Black Panther movement of the 1960s.[23] Although Reichardt claims that "there's no message in this movie" and that she is not a political "joiner," Portland's Occupy movement was a draw for her and Raymond after they finished the script. "We already had the script before Occupy had started up. But it was exciting for these things to be developing at the same time."[24] While Raymond and Reichardt profess to stay on the political margins, Reichardt's long-time producer Neil Kopp had a more personal connection to environmental politics, having come from the north-west and had a childhood friend "who did something pretty radical and went to jail for a long time."[25] Kopp, a sailboat owner, brainstormed the title, and while Reichardt admits *Night Moves* was only intended to be a temporary title, it "worked on so many levels" that they kept it.[26]

HISTORICAL IMPLICATIONS: OKLAHOMA

While on the surface Oklahoma and Oregon do not seem to have a connected history, through Reichardt's film spectators can see multiple parallels. Oklahoma's tourism commission claims the state has the most lake shore mileage of any in the nation, and that might be a reaction from the environmental disaster that defines the area. The 1930s dust bowl ravaged the entire American midwest, but particularly Oklahoma, and "the combination of drought, economic depression, and poor or inappropriate farming practices in the Great Plains led to one of the most serious environmental catastrophes the

United States has ever experienced."[27] As a result the waterways in Oklahoma are almost all fully controlled or man-made, and the state has the "fifth-largest inventory [of dams] in the United States."[28] Both Oregon and Oklahoma use their diverted waterways to provide resources for their residents, but Oklahoma's high level of control over its waterways sets it apart. It seems the memory of want and ecological disaster defines the psyche of an Oklahoma resident and their relationship to water. Unfortunately the dust bowl is not the only disaster that defines Oklahoma and its citizens.

The reason the *Night Moves* trio have trouble buying their explosive material, ammonium nitrate fertilizer, is not lost on an American audience. It is the same explosive that Timothy McVeigh and Terry Nichols used in the 1995 Oklahoma City bombing, which targeted the Alfred P. Murrah federal building. The bomb—a moving truck stuffed with nearly 4,000 pounds of fertilizer—destroyed one-third of the building and killed 168 people, including nineteen children; 680 others were injured.[29] As a direct result of this incident, the Bureau of Alcohol, Tobacco, Firearms and Explosives initiated stricter laws around the purchase of ammonium nitrate fertilizer, such as requirements for buyer identification and maintenance of seller records. In 2011 another piece of legislation proposed by the U.S. Secretary of Homeland Security created the Ammonium Nitrate Security Program, which added more layers of surveillance and regulation for the sale of ammonium nitrate, requiring retailers to report theft or loss of the substance within twenty-four hours and to keep stricter records of purchases.[30] In *Night Moves* Dena is required to show her ID card, but she would not have had to hand over her social security card; and Harmon must have traveled far and wide to buy the "one thousand pounds or so," since each store he bought from will have tracked his purchase. Dena is offered the non-explosive sulfate nitrogen fertilizer that was also a direct result of the Oklahoma domestic terrorism; Sulf-N 26 was developed by Honeywell, a conglomerate company, using research funded by the Department of Homeland Security.[31] By the summer of 1995, Congress required that "chemical taggants" be added to all explosives in an effort to identify where they were manufactured.[32] When Dena looks up at the camera and decides to take her hat off she insures the trio will be caught, since the fertilizer can be traced back to the store from which it was purchased. However, without this act she might not seem trustworthy enough for the store manager to allow the transaction. It is ironic that Dena's convincing explanation for buying the bomb material is that she wants to give life to crops and grass that nourish animals—when, in fact, their plan ultimately takes life away.

Even before the Oklahoma City bombing, ammonium nitrate had a troubled history in many cities across the globe.[33] The substance was outlawed in Afghanistan, since it was made into "bombs against NATO soldiers," and countries such as China, Ireland, and the Philippines have regulated its usage due to its disruptive potential.[34] However, even with this destructive history, the U.S. government has battled multiple times with capitalist roadblocks from those who make a profit on the fertilizer. Just after the Oklahoma City bombing, the victims unsuccessfully sued to have ammonium nitrate "desensitized."[35] If this lawsuit had been successful, Reichardt's band of youthful rebellious environmentalists could not have exploded the dam. While *Night Moves* sheds light on many of the victims' frustrations and fears such as someone being allowed to lay their hands on 1,600 pounds of such a dangerous material—the reality is that alternatives to the fertilizer such as Agrium have become so popular that there are only two main manufacturers in the U.S., and they operate in the south (Arkansas and Mississippi).[36] Dena's suppliers would probably have purchased their ammonium nitrate fertilizer from one of the largest producers in the country, Agrium Inc., whose plant operated in Washington state, but in 2005 the company closed its plants and "the use of ammonium nitrate fertilizer there and in neighboring states plunged . . . farmers quit using it . . . They had alternative nitrogen fertilizers to choose from."[37] In reality, the trio probably could not have found enough explosive fertilizer to create the bomb, simply because they lived in Oregon and not Arkansas. It is no wonder the store employees seem suspicious of Dena from the moment she asks for the substance. Ultimately it is her accusation of sexism that completes the deal, and while spectators do not see the exact transaction, Reichardt allows enough dialogue for them to understand the careful pressure Dena asserts in her argument.

While the intentions of the *Night Moves* characters are completely different from those of the perpetrators of the Oklahoma City bombing, both acts are labeled terroristic. The philosophical questions Reichardt's film raises are extremely timely in light of the twenty-first-century struggle against terrorism and its quest for the root of radicalization for those who commit terror acts.

EARTH LIBERATION FRONT (ELF)

Reichardt often drops audiences directly into the middle of her characters' lives, supplying little to no background information. In *Night Moves* viewers gather small bits of information from dialogue and context clues, learning that Josh is a migrant worker, Dena comes from a privileged lifestyle, and Harmon is ex-military; but nothing that explains their current trajectory. The film poses difficult questions surrounding acts of extremism within environmental movements. A closer examination of movements such as Earth Liberation Front (ELF) might offer a glimpse into how Josh, Dena, and Harmon became radicalized.

Nominated for an Academy Award, and recipient of the 2011 Sundance Film Festival's Best Documentary Editing, Marshall Curry's film *If a Tree Falls: A Story of the Earth Liberation Front* (2011) walks viewers through the history of the Earth First! movement, piecing together news footage and interviews that explore how the ELF movement was born by splintering away from Earth First! in favor of more radicalized action. Through the figure of Daniel McGowan viewers learn about the acts of destruction and arson he and his partners initiated; but unlike the trio in *Night Moves*, McGowan's group drew the line at taking human life. The ELF had designs on destroying property and business interests associated with environmental waste. According to the ELF mission statement on their website, "the ELF's mission is to defend and protect the Earth for future generations by means of direct action."[38] The website goes on to state that "non-violent action is a last resort" and cautions ELF agents to think twice about engaging in property destruction. However, it touts photos of sunken ships and property fires, all presumably ELF targets. An interesting connection is Edward Abbey, who published the novel *The Monkey Wrench Gang* in 1975 and was very active in Earth First! His book, a "how-to" manual for sabotage, was considered inspirational to the founding of the Earth First! movement, and the term "monkey wrenching" was coined to mean "any law-breaking to preserve wilderness, wild spaces and ecosystems."[39] Early in the production of *Night Moves*, Reichardt and her team were sued by Edward Abbey's widow Clarke Abbey, and producer Edward Pressman; the suit claimed, "Raymond and Reichardt copied protectable elements of [*The Monkey Wrench Gang*] in writing *Night Moves* and, since they had no authorization from plaintiffs to do so, they thereby infringed the exclusive rights in the novel afforded to plaintiffs under the Copyright Act."[40] One impetus for the lawsuit may have been the view that Abbey would have objected to Reichardt's decision to show environmentalists (who seem to represent Earth First! members) murder a hiker in their eco-terrorist act. There was no loss of life in either the Earth First! or the ELF acts of sabotage, and the plot twist interjected by Reichardt is, at the very least, unhelpful for the movement. However, another motivation for the lawsuit could have been that the estate was already in talks with Pressman to produce a film based on the book.[41] In his lawsuit, as discussed by Larry Zerner in the *Copyrights and Wrongs* blog, Pressman basically lists just three similarities:

> 1) that both works feature the targeting of a dam for destruction by means of ammonium fertilizer-laden boats, 2) that in both works, the principal bomb maker is a beer guzzling veteran who served overseas, where he acquired his knowledge of explosives, and 3) that both works feature a 20-something woman who starts out as a companion of another member of the group but develops a sexual relationship with the bomb-making

veteran, despite his initial objections to her participation in the group's illegal activities. Now the complaint does state that these similarities are by way of example only, and so there may be many more similarities between the works, but in my experience, if they had more (or better similarities) they would have included them in the complaint. The similarities listed above are not even close to the level of substantial similarity required to prove copyright infringement.[42]

According to Zerner, the case was dismissed soon after being filed, without Reichardt having to "answer the complaint." While the copyright issues were settled, there is no doubt about the connection between existing environmental groups and the protagonists' activities within the events of the film.

Early in *Night Moves*, viewers see a mock environmental documentary directed by Reichardt's longtime collaborator Larry Fessenden. The gathering around this mock documentary introduces audiences to the types of events that might galvanize environmentally concerned members of a community to take "direct action." Dena raises her hand during the documentary's question and answer session, and asks what steps the director suggests citizens take to save the planet. The director suggests a culmination of "small steps" would eventually turn the environmental tide; and the scene cuts quickly to Josh, who is purposefully isolated and quiet, with an intense expression. Of course, viewers know Dena and Josh have already planned their small step to help save the planet's resources, and the exchange serves to positively reaffirm this decision, at least in their minds. When comparing scenes like this one to *If a Tree Falls*, audiences can draw direct associations between the protagonists and Daniel McGowan. While Reichardt abruptly drops viewers into Josh's life and surroundings without providing much context, McGowan's story of radicalization and environmental action offer an example of how someone might reach a similar point. *If a Tree Falls* picks up after McGowan has been put on house arrest. For his acts of terrorism, he is sentenced to seven years in a maximum security prison specifically designed for terrorists. While Curry's film provides historical information in the form of interviews with perpetrators, prosecutors and victims, it seems to signal a broadly sympathetic response toward McGowan and members of the ELF. Like Josh, Dena, and Harmon, they are young, impressionable, and passionate; and while in *Night Moves* we hear from Harmon that a few of the people involved in the last terrorist act were jailed, viewers never learn what radicalized the three main characters. In *If a Tree Falls*, on the other hand, McGowan and other interviewees explain that their turn toward extremism was prompted by a mixture of government and police brutality, and the apparent lack of will from moderate environmental groups. Sean, who operates the organic farm on which Josh works in *Night Moves*, and his farm family appear to represent a more moderate environmental philosophy. Josh, in his efforts to make visible change, only puts pressure on environmentalists who operate in a slower, more systematic way, like Sean or the farmer who burns his cheese license. According to *If a Tree Falls*, some of the final acts of McGowan's team (such as the accidental destruction of Washington State University's library and the false information that led to the burning of SUVs) hurt the reputation of all environmental movemenrts during that era. Like McGowan, Josh also seems to be hindering the more moderate environmental movement's progress and taking attention away from the issues he deems important. Both men's actions are counterproductive. *Night Moves* does not seem to be making a straightforward statement about ecoterrorism versus more moderate environmental activities; instead, as in her other films, Reichardt allows audiences to debate the issues for themselves.

MATERNITY AND POST-FEMINISM

Whether intentionally or not, Reichardt threads maternal, ecofeminist themes through a film about the slow disintegration of the environment and human character. As in *Wendy and Lucy*, viewers get a taste of ecofeminism, with multiple scenes illustrating that those most affected by patriarchal oppression through the destruction of the environment are female. One reason the Green Peter Dam is blown up is to allow salmon, as they swim upstream each year, to spawn (dams block this natural process). From the beginning of the film, audiences are subtly reminded of the core environmental issue motivating the characters. In the opening scene viewers first hear the turbines in the dam, and then see the circular opening of the water release tube slowly spraying water into the river. The release foreshadows the explosion, but it also evokes orgasmic symbolism. When Josh takes a break from working in the fields a few scenes later, he finds a bird's nest dislodged on the ground and very gently places it back in a tree. On the way to Harmon's trailer, Josh and Dena stop to push a dead doe off the road, only to find it was pregnant. Later, as the trio boat toward their evening destination, the camera lingers on two children innocently playing beside the reservoir in a forest of tree stumps. The empty bird's nest, the dead, pregnant doe, and the forest razed to create a dam all underscore the environmental politics woven into Reichardt's films. Individually, these scenes might be an odd fit with a plot-driven drama; but taken together, they imply that all living beings are connected, from birth through to death. When Josh stares down at his callused and dirty hands after returning to Harmon's trailer with dinner, audiences are reminded that these are the same hands that grow plants and secure birds' nests as well as create bombs and taking life. Reichardt might be implicating viewers through this POV shot, implying that

Figure 8.4 Josh and Surprise mix fertilizer

the misuse of natural resources plays a role in fostering extremism. Josh seems to be questioning his own ability to follow through with their destructive plan as the camera pauses on his hands. Another scene that implies environmental connections is the 180-degree pan in Josh's yurt the morning after the dam explosion. Beginning with a forest view from his window, the camera pans his walls, ultimately connecting nature to humans as it settles on Josh, half smiling, looking up at a sunny day through the circular opening in his ceiling. Like the bird's nest and doe scenes, this cyclical slow pan seems to imply that humans and animals alike are connected and violence affects them equally. In a later scene reminiscent of the bomb mixing, Josh and Surprise are mixing plant fertilizer against the backdrop of mountain foothills (Figure 8.4). The scene serves no purpose other than to impress upon viewers that the same substance and processes can either give or take life, depending on the intention.

While Dena's work symbolizes a maternal sanctuary where women can be free of all constraints, the spa is used for a variety of purposes within the film. In line with the maternal thread, the spa evokes visions of water births creating a nurturing space in a masculine world. As with the image of Cozy in her tub at the beginning of *River of Grass*, viewers are held accountable for their voyeurism—as is Josh ,who on his spa visit uncomfortably closes the wooden door by the outdoor tubs as nude women stroll into and out of baths, seemingly undisturbed by peeping eyes. One function of a spa is to bring about change and renewal for its customers—but ironically this is the site of Dena's murder, a contaminating act by a male outsider.

Dena is the most prominent female character in *Night Moves*, and her character seems problematic and complex from the beginning. While she is not the central protagonist, she is essential to the plot and serves to develop all the characters with whom she interacts. Dena has a post-feminist sensibility; she views herself as an equal in a post-sexist society even though it is clear that Harmon, at least, believes she is unnecessary for the operation. In the few moments of background revelation that Reichardt allows, viewers realize Dena has cast off intellectual pursuits (stating that college is for greedy capitalists who simply want the appearance of an education) and opted instead for a "back to nature" lifestyle. In an effort to get her way, she exploits the issue of gender inequality as a convenient way to purchase the fertilizer, and inserts herself into the masculine world of bomb-making through her ability to provide funds. In fact, she uses money to assert her value throughout most of the film, illustrating the post-feminist idea that women can buy equal rights in a modern society. After choosing to sleep alone in the *Night Moves* boat, specifically in the "cradle of death" (the space that is later packed with explosives, which foreshadows her fate), she has sex with Harmon, knowing they have pledged "no contact" after the event. Like many cinematic women who dare to display independence and sexuality, Dena is fatally punished. Her complexity works to keep audiences from directly identifying with her character, even though she has the most humane reaction to the loss of life.

A CHARACTER STUDY

Throughout most of the film Josh is seen without his fellow collaborators, but when Josh, Dena, and Harmon are together, audiences see the in-depth character study that Reichardt has stated was the main impetus for the film. As in all her work, Reichardt creates character studies, and *Night Moves* is no exception: "I'm far more interested in the inherent drama of everyday life, the small beats you're constantly up against. It's more comfortable territory for me."[43] While planning and executing ecoterrorism is not an ordinary life act, the human interactions surrounding such an act are explored, especially in the breakfast scene before Dena's risky purchase of nitrate fertilizer. This breakfast, one of the scenes with the most shared dialogue, establishes the trio's internal dynamics. The scene opens as Harmon apologizes for wasting time by lack of planning, and a tense and brooding Josh sits staring at his uneaten food (Figure 8.5). Harmon's oversights are quickly adding up, since the morning errand revolves around his inability to buy the fertilizer or communicate this failing to his partners. Dena and Harmon eat with no reservations and even tease each other, but this is quickly cut short as Josh quizzes Dena on her cover story for buying the fertilizer. Josh interrupts Dena to stop the friendly banter, and while this illustrates his nervous short fuse, it may also indicate jealousy. In an earlier scene,

Figure 8.5 At a group breakfast, Harmon apologizes for his oversight

when Dena questioned Harmon's ability and trustworthiness, Josh answered in a defensive, almost aggressive tone that Harmon was "trained by the best—the United States marines." Josh habitually protects Harmon from Dena's questions or stern words by redirecting, silencing, or minimizing her concerns. He privileges Harmon, deferring to his opinions to guide him, while no such deference is given to Dena. Audiences are pelted with Harmon's screw-ups: withholding a criminal record, being recognized in public, booking a crowded campground, being unable to stop the explosion countdown—and Josh tolerates it all. Perhaps his lack of judgment is a plot device, as it drives the action and adds tension, but it also highlights Josh's emotional attachment to Harmon. Josh's emotions are fleeting, since he is extremely reserved and works hard to keep himself tightly wound. In the last conversation he has with Harmon it is unclear whether Josh intends to tie up loose ends, as he did with Dena, or whether he truly wants to "get lost" with Harmon. But no matter where the relationships end up, the breakfast scene establishes Josh's preferences.

Food, especially breakfast, functions to bring the characters together for extended debate. Another significant breakfast scene takes place the morning after Josh returns from his act of ecoterrorism. Reichardt uses this morning conversation to debate all sides of the Oregon environmental water crisis. Josh learns that their actions have led to the unintended death of a camper who was sleeping on the bank of the river, and as we see his initial shock the scene allows audiences a window into his emotional state. Sean, who is a father figure to Josh, openly banters with his two farmhands, Dylan and Surprise, disagreeing with the dam destruction: "They [activists] are idiots

. . . one dam, who cares. That river had ten dams on it. The grid is everywhere. You have to take down 12–100 dams to make a difference . . . It's a statement, right. I'm not interested in a statement; I'm interested in results . . . I call that theatre." In thirty seconds, Josh's political and philosophical beliefs are crushed by a man he clearly respects. Instead of framing the ecological debate around hydroelectric dams and spawning salmon pre-explosion, Reichardt gives viewers a more well-rounded perspective post-explosion to heighten the tension. Spectators have identified with Josh and his cause, only to realize he may have been too hasty in action and thought. While Dylan's mantra is the basis of the first portion of the film—"Someone's got to start somewhere"—it is in this breakfast scene that *Night Moves* shifts philosophical perspectives. Sean points out alternatives such as nuclear power plants, which no one at the table finds acceptable; and then he points toward his own political statement, his farm: "Look out the window; it's a lot slower but it makes a lot more sense to me." Viewers wonder if the farmer's statement is meant to echo Reichardt's own beliefs about handling the environmental issues in Oregon. In an interview with IndieWire, Reichardt hints at her political intent: "[A] variety of options are laid on the table from different characters . . . all trying to be some kind of pull against the destruction of the planet . . . If this more radical approach is the wrong approach, what is the right one? Are any of the things that any of those people [do] enough?"[44] It seems that questioning the ethics of the characters' actions is not the political focus of the film, so much as simply exploring the options for protest. Reichardt submerges audiences in an outsiders' frustrations until this breakfast scene, where audiences hear the variety of activist options available from a local's point of view. Josh, after all, is a migrant worker who might only be passing through, but viewers are not sure, since they are only given hints to his background. Local or not, Josh's time at the farm is at an end, and the second breakfast scene after the dam explosion drives this reality home. Though the scene mirrors the first breakfast scene in scope and location, it is very different in tone and intention: no one makes eye contact with Josh, nor do they talk to each other. The atmosphere is tense, and when Josh lightheartedly says "Hey," none of the characters look up from their activity. No one present condones the ecoterrorism Josh deemed appropriate, and now his politics has endangered the farm. The breakfast scene is reminiscent of several ending scenes from Curry's *If a Tree Falls*, when an older and more regretful Daniel McGowan admits he did not think about the impact his actions would have on his friends and family. The film focuses especially on McGowan's sister, and how her efforts have drained her emotional and economic reserves. For viewers familiar with both films, Josh can be compared with a younger McGowan in that they share the same fate. Josh, like McGowan, will be captured, and his actions will reverberate though the liberal Oregon community that has offered him temporary shelter.

The ending of *Night Moves* seems less hopeful and more cynical than those of Reichardt's previous films. Closest in content to *River of Grass* (minus the dark humor), this ending reinforces the main political message of the film: that capitalism is destroying the environment. Reichardt could have ended the film with Josh throwing out his cell phone in an effort to "get real lost;" instead she opts not only to keep viewers uncomfortable and tense, but to remind them of the seeming impossibility of changing Western environmental behavior. Images like the dancing cow outside a supermarket, the boat owner's excessive home, the family tying canoes to their SUV during the trio's breakfast scene, and an outdoor retailer store at the end all convey the message that capitalism is thriving, even if Oregon's river systems and salmon are not. In their brief phone call, Harmon suggests that Josh needs to "get real lost and stay lost" after learning that Dena "quit on them." Brushing tears away in his first sign of outward emotion apart from paranoia, frustration, or anger, Josh glances up and sees everyday life happening around him—a man walking into a store, trees moving in the wind—and it underscores the fact that although his life is falling apart, the world doesn't stop. Reichardt seems to be reminding spectators that even in the wake of ecological disasters or acts of large-scale terror, everyday events continue.

Even Josh, an outsider who has gone to extremes to "get people to start thinking," has to survive; and that means employment in a system that harms the environment. As he looks down at a job application—which requires an address, something he no longer has—the words of Wally, the security guard from *Wendy and Lucy*, seem applicable: "You can't get an address without an address. You can't get a job without a job. It's all fixed." Wally is discussing poverty and class issues, but capitalist policy has historically been problematic for both the environmental and economic crises in America. Josh hesitates in filling out the application, realizing he has no address and cannot give his real name; and as he looks up to gaze into the reflective security mirror, which might harbor a surveillance camera, viewers see two women shopping with a phone in one hand and what appears to be a Starbucks drink in another. These details further reinforce the point that even though Josh has blown up a dam to "save the planet," he cannot really make a difference, or even a dent. Capitalism, just as in *Wendy and Lucy*, is simply too strong a force. Though many of Reichardt's characters seem lost at the end of her films—Cozy aimlessly driving, Kurt emotionally and physically directionless, Wendy huddled alone in a boxcar, Emily confronting a waterless desert; the multiple protagonists in *Certain Women* are arguably her most settled characters—Josh leaves viewers hopeless. He has missed Sean's message of combating capitalism slowly, through small changes, and now he finds himself helpless to make any real changes, whether to himself or to the environment. Josh signifies an utterly bleak message about our environment and about his well-being. His extremism has not solved any environmental problems; it has served only to put pressure on others around him who could create systematic change.

NOTES

1. Reichardt quoted in Melina Gills, "Kelly Reichardt On Directing 'Night Moves,' Editing Her Own Films, and Shooting in Living Spaces," *IndieWire*, 30 May 2014, <http://www.indiewire.com/2014/05/kelly-reichardt-on-directing-night-moves-editing-her-own-films-and-shooting-in-living-spaces-25945/> (accessed 20 September 2017).
2. "*Night Moves* (2013): Awards," *Internet Movie Database*, <http://www.imdb.com/title/tt2043933/awards?ref_=tt_awd> (accessed 20 September 2017).
3. "*Night Moves*," *Box Office Mojo*, <http://www.boxofficemojo.com/movies/?id=nightmoves.htm> (accessed 20 September 2017).
4. Ibid.
5. Eugene Hernandez, "Kelly Reichardt Q&A: *Night Moves*" (Film Society of Lincoln Center interview, 31 July 2014), <https://www.youtube.com/watch?v=18zzyN9FRew> (accessed 20 September 2017).
6. Ibid.
7. Ibid.
8. Ibid.
9. Ibid.
10. Ibid.
11. Ibid.
12. Ibid.
13. Ibid.
14. Jon Silberg, "Spotlight: Christopher Blauvelt," *Digital Video* 22, no. 6 (2014): 16, <http://www.creativeplanetnetwork.com/news/orphaned-articles/spotlight-christopher-blauvelt-cinematographer-night-moves/605620> (accessed 20 September 2017).
15. "Kelly Reichardt Q&A: *Night Moves*."
16. Ibid.
17. Ibid.
18. Ibid.
19. Ibid.
20. Erin Marie Arizzi, "Modeling Professional Femininity Through U.S. Media Culture, 1963–2015" (Ph.D. dissertation, 2015), <http://search.proquest.com/docview/1755656600/>, pp. 177–8 (accessed 20 September 2017).
21. Ibid. p. 203.
22. "Occupy Wall Street: A Protest Timeline," *The Week*, 21 July 2016, <http://theweek.com/articles/481160/occupy-wall-street-protest-timeline> (accessed 20 September 2017).
23. Peter Rugh, "Building a Radical Environmental Movement, " *Occupy Wall Street*, <http://occupywallstreet.net/story/building-radical-environmental-movement> (accessed 20 September 2017).
24. David Jenkins and Nick James, "The Dam Busters," *Sight & Sound* 24, no. 9 (2014): 56–9; *International Bibliography of Theatre & Dance* (accessed 1 June 2016).
25. Jenkins and James, "Dam Busters."

26. Ibid.

27. Donald A. Wilhite, "Dust Bowl," *The Encyclopedia of Oklahoma History and Culture*, <http://www.okhistory.org/publications/enc/entry.php?entry=du011> (accessed 20 September 2017).

28. Joe Wertz, "Mapped: Oklahoma's Dams and the Potential Hazards They Pose," *State Impact*, 12 December 2014, <https://stateimpact.npr.org/oklahoma/2014/12/12/mapped-oklahomas-dams-and-the-potential-hazards-they-pose/> (accessed 20 September 2017).

29. "Victims of the Oklahoma City Bombing," *USA Today*, 20 June 2001, <https://usatoday30.usatoday.com/news/nation/2001-06-11-mcveigh-victims.htm> (accessed 20 September 2017).

30. Office of the Press Secretary, "Secretary Napolitano Announces Proposed Ammonium Nitrate Security Program" (Washington: Department of Homeland Security, 2011), <https://www.dhs.gov/news/2011/08/02/secretary-napolitano-announces-proposed-ammonium-nitrate-security-program> (accessed 20 September 2017).

31. Associated Press, "Company Creates Hard-to-Ignite Fertilizer to Foil Bomb-Makers," *Fox News*, 23 September 2008, <http://www.foxnews.com/story/2008/09/23/company-creates-hard-to-ignite-fertilizer-to-foil-bomb-makers.html?sPage=fnc/scitech/naturalscience> (accessed 20 September 2017).

32. Jerry Gray, "Senate Votes to Aid Tracing of Explosives," *The New York Times*, 6 June 1995, <http://www.nytimes.com/1995/06/06/us/senate-votes-to-aid-tracing-of-explosives.html> (accessed 20 September 2017).

33. Steve Thompson and Reese Dunklin, "Ammonium Nitrate Sold by Ton as U.S. Regulation Is Stymied," *The Dallas Morning News*, October 2013, <https://www.dallasnews.com/news/news/2013/10/05/ammonium-nitrate-sold-by-ton-as-u.s.-regulation-is-stymied> (accessed 20 September 2017).

34. Ibid.

35. Ibid.

36. Ibid.

37. Ibid.

38. Earth Liberation Front, history and photo gallery, <http://earth-liberation-front.com/> (accessed 17 April 2017).

39. "The Monkey Wrench Gang," *Wikipedia*, <https://en.wikipedia.org/w/index.php?title=The_Monkey_Wrench_Gang&oldid=754557508> (accessed 17 April 2017).

40. Dominic Patten, "'Night Moves' Director, Producers, UTA Sued By Edward Pressman & Edward Abbey Widow For Copyright Infringement," *Deadline Hollywood*, 15 September 2012, <http://deadline.com/2012/09/uta-director-kelly-reichardt-sued-by-edward-pressman-edward-abbey-widow-for-copyright-infringement-336968/> (accessed 20 September 2017).

41. Ibid.

42. "The Monkey Business in the 'Monkey Wrench' Copyright Infringement Lawsuit," *Copyrights and Wrongs* (blog), 16 September 2012, <https://zernerlaw.wordpress.com/2012/09/16/the-monkey-business-in-the-monkey-wrench-copyright-infringement-lawsuit/> (accessed 20 September 2017).

43. Reichardt quoted in Iain Blair, "Variety Honoree Kelly Reichardt: Still on the Side of the Outsiders," *Variety Online*, 20 January 2016, <http://variety.com/2016/film/festivals/variety-honoree-kelly-reichardt-still-on-the-side-of-the-outsiders-1201683518/> (accessed 20 September 2017).

44. Reichardt quoted in Gills, "Kelly Reichardt on Directing 'Night Moves.'"

CHAPTER 9

Solidification: *Certain Women*

Insiders are already well-covered ... I'm far more interested in the inherent drama of everyday life, the small beats you're constantly up against. —Kelly Reichardt[1]

In the tradition of Kelly Reichardt's earlier work, *Certain Women* explores lost and isolated characters who are content to remain outsiders or on the margins. Adapted from short stories by Maile Meloy, the film is divided into three episodes, with a focus on working women and their relationships. While the plots loosely interconnect, they all center on female protagonists. Laura (Laura Dern) is a lawyer wrangling a volatile client; Gina (Michelle Williams) is a successful entrepreneur struggling to find balance within her family; and Jamie, a Native American rancher (Lily Gladstone) is battling isolation and infatuation with her teacher, Beth Travis (Kristen Stewart). Reichardt's cinematic auteur characteristics are all showcased in *Certain Women*, as is her thought-provoking social commentary. The expansive Montana landscapes and barren winter setting reflect the emotional state of the characters, and Reichardt's minimalism creates an authentic portrayal of a flawed, complex, and vulnerable humanity.

PRODUCTION

Just a few months after wrapping *Night Moves* (2013), Reichardt received the news that Sony Pictures Worldwide Acquisitions' Stage 6 Films had purchased international distribution rights to the untitled project that would later be unveiled as *Certain Women*.[2] She worked on adapting the script for a year and a half before that purchase jump-started production. IFC bought domestic rights after the film premiered at the 2016 Sundance Film Festival, and its theatrical release was in mid-October. *Certain Women* is Reichardt's most financially successful film to date, having grossed more than one million dollars at the box office.[3] Around fifty crew members worked on location during the thirty-day film shoot, with an estimated two-million-dollar budget (also her largest to date).[4] Reichardt scouted in Oregon, Idaho, and Montana before settling on Livingston, Montana because the state gave tax incentives and a grant to the production. Meloy's short stories are set throughout Montana, and its landscapes, like those of Oregon, allowed Reichardt plenty of scope to depict working-class characters in a striking setting. During her scouting trips Reichardt met people who informed her characterizations, and she also drew ideas from the locations. On one trip, she learned about the daily processes of ranching by shadowing a sixty-one-year-old woman rancher who lived alone and worked with twenty horses.[5] While the character of Jamie in *Certain Women* is much younger and seems to be working in a seasonal job as a rancher, the level of detail during the scenes in which she cares for her horses illustrates how closely Reichardt studied the lifestyle. Montana was blanketed in snow during the majority of the scouting trips, and Reichardt anticipated shooting a film that would look very white. By March, temperatures had dropped significantly, making outside filming brutal—but contrary to expectations, there was little to no snow. This prompted Reichardt to rethink her camera choices and shoot in 16mm.[6]

Composer Jeff Grace (*Meek's Cutoff*, *Night Moves*) again worked with Reichardt, and while the majority of the film uses source sounds and silence, his score swells profoundly toward the end. Kent Sparling, the sound designer who collaborated on *Night Moves*, worked with Reichardt at Skywalker Ranch during the five-to-six-month editing process;[7] she also made use of the editing facilities at the Wexner Center after being selected for its $50,000 Artist in Residency Award.[8] From beginning to end *Certain Women* seems to gradually become more and more silent, which reflects Reichardt's methods on set; shooting scenes with dialogue first, and then reshooting them without words to allow gestures, emotions, or the actors' physicality to create tension.[9] The technique of using camera placement, landscape, or a lens change to convey plot instead of relying on dialogue is something audiences have come to expect from Reichardt's work, as are the lost and lonely protagonists she depicts.

ADAPTATION: LOST CHARACTERS AND OPEN ENDINGS

Adaptation criticism has historically focused on fidelity—how closely a film follows its literary origins—but many contemporary theorists, such as Linda Hutcheon, counter that adaptation interpretation involves:

multi-layered application, referring simultaneously to (a) the entity or product which is the result of transposing a particular source, (b) the process through which the entity or product was created (including reinterpretation and re-creation of the source), and (c) the process of reception . . . the ways in which we [the audience] associate the entity or product as both similar to and a departure from the original.[10]

Reichardt's goal for *Certain Women* seems to lie in representing the daily life of working-class people who experience isolation. Her adaptation of Meloy's stories creates that opportunity, and allows audiences to revisit the literary characters cinematically. Adaptation theorist Robert Stam situates the debate by suggesting that audiences "consider a film adaptation not as a direct translation of its source into a new medium, but as a new work of art that has a dialogic relationship with its source—that is, the film becomes one of many possible readings of the film, not an attempt to convey the 'one true meaning' of a book."[11] Through her slow cinematic and minimalist style, Reichardt gives audiences the opportunity to digest the cinematic "new work of art" and add their own interpretations, an auteur characteristic that is prevalent in all her films. When adapting Maile Meloy's short stories Reichardt sets aside concerns with fidelity to instead create an adaptation that enriches the women's lives, effectively complicating their realistic portrayal. Reichardt creates opportunities for each of her episodes to overlap, and while this does necessitate some revisions to the plots of Meloy's stories, it serves to tighten the overarching themes of the film and the characters' relationships.

The characters in *Certain Women* are all, without exception, lost and isolated. Even the town of Livingston, a loose thread that ties the characters together, seems lonely and bleak. The film opens with a whistling train reminiscent of Wendy in *Wendy and Lucy* (2008) huddled alone in a boxcar, and the bleak mountainous landscape recalls the harsh desert Emily navigates in *Meek's Cutoff* (2010). All Reichardt's characters struggle with internal issues; *Old Joy's* (2004) protagonist Mark is working through his role as a new father, while Josh's paranoia in *Night Moves* (2013) offers little hope of redemption. The protagonists of *Certain Women* are arguably in somewhat less dire straits than these earlier examples, as the film's epilogue illustrates. A striking similarity between Meloy's writing style and Reichardt's visual storytelling is the way social and political commentary are subtly worked into the characters' daily existence. As well as addressing issues of class, race, age, labor, and family, Reichardt cinematically embellishes one pivotal sentence in each episode written by Meloy addressing feminist concerns. While Reichardt honors many elements of Meloy's stories, these choices make *Certain Women* fit her own vision as expressed by her filmography.

Reichardt bypasses mainstream chronological and linear storytelling in *Certain Women* by presenting three mostly independent episodes with detached epilogues. The first is based on the short story "Tome" from Meloy's book *Half in Love: Stories.* The original story features an unnamed female lawyer and her client; Reichardt gives the lawyer a name, Laura, and the film begins with her male client, Fuller, questioning her competency until a male co-worker concurs with her judgment. Reichardt captures most of what Meloy writes when the lawyer states: "That's what it's like to be a man. If I were a man I could explain the law and people would listen and say, 'Okay.' It would be so restful."[12] The fact that readers never learn the narrator's name in Meloy's story reiterates her seeming invisibility within a male-dominated profession. Early scenes indicate potential catharsis, as her story begins with an affair and hostage entanglement; however, both situations ultimately fizzle out. In *Certain Women*, Laura's affair is clearly dull, as indicated by the bland painted walls of the motel. When her lover calls to break off the relationship Laura is not granted time to finish the conversation, but she does not seem overly concerned. Reichardt gives audiences just enough information to follow along in the moment, and the narrative technique is engrossing. When Laura arrives at the scene of a hostage situation and receives bad advice from Sherriff Rowles, audiences expect the worst for her as she enters the building. However, in true Reichardt form, those expectations are blunted and less dramatic, more realistic events unfold. When Laura visits a previous client in jail—a client who held her hostage during the first segment of the film—their conversation indicates she is still, as before, uninterested in and unaffected by his behavior.

Ironically, Laura's client, after taking her hostage in a failed attempt at justice, writes to her from jail reassuring her not to feel bad that she was unable to help him flee the police: "and don't feel too bad about what happened. Of course they [police] were out front. You did what you could do."[13] The assumption that a lawyer would feel guilty about not aiding and abetting a fugitive, one who took her hostage at gunpoint, seems comical, but might explain the variance in tone during Laura's visit. Meloy's short story openly acknowledges that the lawyer's visit is awkward and her gift of food feels "heavy and wrong," but in *Certain Women* Reichardt allows her audience to impose their own interpretation on the appropriateness and tone of the visit. Reichardt layers her episodes by turning portions of Meloy's short stories into epilogues. In the lawyer's case it is the jail visit that ends her story, and Reichardt flips Meloy's ending to the opening scene. Meloy's lawyer finds a lover who is identified as "a prosecutor who never left the office before midnight," with no indication that this person is someone else's husband, or even connected to another short story.[14] In Reichardt's film, introducing an identifiable lover—Gina's husband—into the Laura storyline works on many different levels; audiences now see a direct connection between the first two episodes, and on a production note, a call from her lover keeps Laura in her car and occupied long enough for her angry client to jump into her car. The addition also contributes to audiences' interpretation of both Laura and Gina.

The second episode of *Certain Women* is adapted from the short story "Native Sandstone," also found in *Half in Love: Stories*. It centers around businesswoman Gina, who successfully acquires sandstone from the property of a retired neighbor, Albert. Meloy's character is more sympathetic than the cinematic Gina, because her characterization is more complex and flawed in Reichardt's adaptation. Viewers glimpse the challenges she encounters as a wife and as a mother to a seemingly spoiled but emotionally neglected teenage daughter, Guthrie (Sara Rodier). Gina negotiates a tense relationship with both her daughter and her husband, Ryan, who audiences recognize as Laura's lover. Reichardt relies on patriarchal cultural codes that prompt audiences to question the priorities of working mothers, especially those who appear ambitious. One scene effectively illustrates these biased assumptions when Albert examines Ryan's business card and seems confused about his position. Ryan motions to a distant Gina, saying, "She's a boss," suggesting that they work together and he reports to her. By complicating the central character, Reichardt creates audience accountability to and awareness of gender bias. Spectators assume Gina's ambition has driven her husband into Laura's arms and alienated her daughter. When Ryan leans toward the disgruntled daughter, Guthrie, and tells her to go easy on her mother because "she does a lot for us," Reichardt is again allowing viewers to add their own interpretation of the family's back story with only a few words.

While spectators work to understand Gina and her family dynamics, Meloy paints a different picture of the central character, including subtle gender commentary that may have inspired Reichardt's character adaptation. The interactions between Albert and Ryan highlight male communication and trust-building, sometimes relying on the exclusion of women. Meloy addresses this when her character reluctantly initiates the request for sandstone, knowing it would be better received if coming from her husband: "[Gina] wasn't ready to abandon their purpose but she did wish [Ryan] would ask. Men turned to [Ryan], they trusted him. He did what he said he would; that was why she had married him."[15] Like the other cinematic episodes, this storyline is also about loneliness and lack—there is clearly respect within the marriage, but not much affection. It seems that the sandstone is a "freestanding monument" glorifying a patriarchal past, one with a clear and well-defined social hierarchy that kept women and native people in their place. Ryan states that Gina wants to use "authentic" materials to build their house, hence the sandstone; but as the film unfolds, spectators realize that while Gina is obsessed with being authentic, she is ultimately lost and seems misplaced in her environment. Much like the sandstone, which was compromised and shaped by pioneer hands to build a schoolhouse, Gina struggles with her surroundings and with the relationship compromises required to keep her life in place.

Meloy depicts a central character who is extremely knowledgeable about Albert, indicating multiple visits and a solid relationship; Reichardt leaves enough space during the scenes between Albert and Gina to create doubt as to Gina's good intentions beyond obtaining the object of her desire. It is clear that the couple have visited Albert many times, as Meloy's businesswoman character knows many details about his life and preferences. These details (much like the specificity of Wendy's thoughts as she shops in the supermarket in *Wendy and Lucy*) are not disclosed to the viewer as they are to the reader. Meloy makes it clear that her character knows Albert's bluegrass band is called the Catfish; she knows he thinks Russian olive trees make good shade; and she is aware he "didn't dislike Mormons." Her desire to bring him something useful, mixed with her sadness at taking his stone, creates a more sympathetic characterization in Meloy's story than Reichardt allows on screen.

Gina's ending, as compared with the other two episodes, reveals more change than those of her counterparts. During the epilogue she smokes openly, as opposed to an earlier stamping out of a private cigarette, and seems genuinely happy—for the moment—with her recent stone acquisitions. Reichardt seems to present a questionable family dynamic without casting judgement or being didactic. All three members of Gina's family are disconnected, with no clear sign of imminent change. Although Ryan has ended his affair with Laura and tells Guthrie to be nice to her mother, these changes seem superficial. In the end, it is the landscape that suggests longer-term inner change for Gina: the sun is shining, the family is surrounded by friends and possibly family, and Gina seems to crack a genuine smile. Reichardt depicts her as a flawed woman who, like the native desert plants she wants for her new home, has mastered the art of survival in a complicated and sometimes harsh environment.

The final episode of *Certain Women* is arguably the most intense and emotionally gripping of the three. This is due in part to its slow cinematic characteristics, but also because the central character radiates a wrenching desire for companionship. Jamie works on a horse ranch, and for much of her screen time she is immersed in the daily processes of caring for the livestock and for herself. Meloy's title for the original story adapted here is the name of the school law teacher: "Travis, B." The name is listed as it appears in the phone directory because in the short story the protagonist looks up the teacher's phone number; but Reichardt leaves those details out of her screen adaptation. It is happenstance that Jamie decides to stop one night at her local high school to attend classes and meets Beth Travis, with whom she feels a strong connection. The rancher is shown as highly competent at caring for horses and for the land, even as her broken wrist signals that what she does is physically demanding; yet she exhibits few skills in navigating social situations. The most obvious and significant adjustment from the short story to the film is the protagonist's change in gender: the rancher in Meloy's version is a young man whose polio battle has left him with a misplaced right hip. Meloy's readers move from a subjective point of view, guided by internal monologue, to an objective one, shut out of the rancher's thoughts. This objective point of view allows Kristen Stewart to better own her character, giving Beth a harder edge than the story indicates, since film audiences are left to interpret Beth without the aid of Jamie's thoughts. In Meloy's story, when Beth is delivered back to her car following the horse ride, the rancher cuts Beth off: "She started to say something, but in his nervousness he cut her off. 'See you Thursday,' he said." Later, he laments this action: "He should have let her say what she wanted to say."[16] In the short story, readers learn that Beth was about to tell the rancher that she had asked for a Glendive teaching replacement, and this admission might have saved him the drive to Missoula. Beth even softens the blow as they recount that earlier moment in the parking lot toward the end of the story: "'It wasn't because—' she said. 'I meant to tell you on Tuesday.'"[17] Within the short story, Beth tries to reassure him that he was not the reason she requested a replacement; but Reichardt strategically cuts actions and words like these from the script, allowing space for viewer interpretation.

Meloy's story incorporates many heteronormative romantic signifiers that are absent from Reichardt's adaptation. The cultural signs of male sexual exploration are interspersed throughout the short story and the associated aggressive behavior is replaced with an emphasis on loneliness: "he had some girlie magazines that he got to know better than he'd ever known an actual person."[18] As the rancher finishes his second class, other heteronormative signs appear: "he had assumed, for forty-eight hours, that he would go to dinner with her, but now he didn't know how to make that happen. He had never asked any girl anywhere. There had been girls in high school who had felt sorry for him, but he had been too shy or too proud to take advantage of it."[19] Meloy delivers a male character who views women as something to be acted upon, but one who does not follow through, at least not until he meets Beth: "He wished he had practiced, with the high school girls or the friendly secretaries, just to be ready for this moment . . . He caught up her hand again and kissed it, because he had wanted to do that . . . Then he leaned over and kissed her cheek, because he had wanted to do that, too."[20] Readers and audiences find the protagonist sympathetic, but on a basic level it is impossible to escape the fact that the story entails stalking, or at the very least, obsessive behavior. Personal boundaries become important, and a larger picture of female autonomy materializes. While Meloy's character kisses Beth with no warning, he does later illustrate appropriate awareness of boundaries and self-control, serving as an example in a contemporary society that pushes aggressive sexualized masculinity. He "shove[s] his hands into his jeans" when he wants to touch Beth, and acknowledges the "protective look the man in the dark suit had given her" during their parking-lot conversation.[21] He also does "what he knew he should do" and throws away Beth's phone number, as if modeling appropriate behavior after a rejection. Nevertheless, and no matter the gender, a nine-hour drive, six hundred miles one way, to Missoula is the elephant in the room.

Reichardt revises the story to capture an unrequited lesbian infatuation; however, true to her style, she makes writing and directing choices that allow audiences to interpret the relationship in multiple ways. Many actions in the original story are cut so that Reichardt can develop the relationship between two women instead of the short story's heteronormative version. Jamie does not kiss Beth in *Certain Women*, and viewers can only guess what she is thinking behind her expressive eyes. Personal boundaries seem to be implicit from the beginning, unlike with Meloy's rancher. Jamie makes no attempt to keep Beth's phone number, and a co-worker's glance radiates a question rather than a concern. In fact, Jamie's hesitation could be chalked up to social anxiety and a longing for friendship as opposed to romantic sentiment. Lily Gladstone uses emotional repression and restraint to create a sympathetic characterization; her loneliness become tangible as her daily routine is shown through moving images. Jamie's episode begins and ends with her feeding, grooming, and exercising horses. Audiences become familiar with her duties as they watch her multiple trips in an all-terrain vehicle to deliver hay to a snow-blanketed field, while her dogs run and play in the deep snow tracks left behind. The use of silence and source sound combines with the meticulous depiction of the business of surviving a Montana winter, driving home Jamie's isolation. Reichardt was conscious of the need to balance her character's emotional state; having taken enough footage of Gladstone working with the horses to create an additional film, she suggests in an interview that "the beauty of the place overwhelms the roughness of the chore, and so it kind of cancels it."[22] Meloy's short story indicates a danger associated with this isolation, citing mental health concerns: "He got afraid of himself that winter; he sensed something dangerous that would break free if he kept so much alone."[23] Reichardt focuses more on the ranching lifestyle and routine, allowing the visual repetition and open landscape to speak volumes. Instead of reading "girlie magazines," Jamie watches science shows; rather than a gait noticeably affected by a stiff, painful hip, she has an arm cast. Meloy's rancher feels his isolation enveloping him, and so searches out interaction at the school; Reichardt leaves Jamie's intentions ambiguous, relying on context clues to inform viewers as they watch her dress and drive into town, slowing near the high school and ultimately finding a seat in the back of the classroom. While the class serves as a mechanism for Jamie and Beth to meet, it also provides an opportunity for Reichardt to highlight issues of race, class, and educational opportunity.

In her short story, Meloy brings attention to the social injustices suffered by Native Americans at the hands of the American educational system, but Reichardt only offers visual clues. Jamie seems uncomfortable in the school setting, and her family stories seem to leave out much discussion of education. Race and social justice is a recurring topic throughout the film as well as in the short story, especially since education and white-collar jobs belong to those who are white (Beth and many of the other teachers) and Jamie is Native American, working a manual labor job. Discrepancies in opportunity are more apparent in the short story, as the school law class begins and readers learn the rancher and his mother had been discriminated against: "He'd never imagined a student had any rights. His mother had grown up in the mission school in St. Xavier, where the Indian kids were beaten for not speaking English, or for no reason. He'd been luckier. An English teacher had once struck him on the head with a dictionary, and a math teacher had splintered a yardstick on his desk."[24] While these thoughts are not referenced in the film, the Catholic missionary school creates a connection with *Meek's Cutoff* and its association with the ideology of manifest destiny. Native American imagery and historical references can be seen throughout Reichardt's films, from the title and opening monologue in *River of Grass* to the subject matter of *Meek's Cutoff*. All three episodes of *Certain Women* hint at First Nation participation, from the dancing Native American group in the mall where Laura Dern eats her lunch to the character of Jamie, whose counterpart in Meloy's story is described as "three-quarters Cheyenne." Lily Gladstone herself is Native American—born in Montana, in the same hospital as Michelle Williams—and lived on reservations until she was eleven years old.[25] It is also plausible that the pioneer-etched sandstone Gina craves in her episode is the remnants of a school with a history of racial bias.

While Jamie's fate during the epilogue of the third installment seems less optimistic than the others, she is safely back in her comfort zone, feeding horses in the barn. Of all the women, the rancher seems to take the most emotional risk, but with no visible consequences. Her decision to drive for four hours and sleep all night in frigid temperatures simply to say hello to Beth illustrates movement, but to no avail. Jamie is heartbreakingly thrust back into her daily routine, and audiences are left watching her tend to her animals while a talk radio program incidentally discusses high school dropouts. Much like all Reichardt's characters, the protagonists of *Certain Women* maintain their status quo, even if not deliberately.

In both the short stories and the film the Montana landscape, particularly the town of Livingston, becomes a character. The town is the setting for the first episode, but it is referenced in all three episodes, with Ryan wearing a Livingston hat and Beth driving the four-hour stretch from Livingston to Glendive, as opposed to the nine hours from Missoula. Just as the landscape of the Oregon desert was framed by restrictive sunbonnets to create a claustrophobic feeling in *Meek's Cutoff*, Reichardt explains, the Montana landscape contributed to the feel of *Certain Women*: "There are mountains on all sides of you, which in many ways locks you in, and I think changes the way you look at the world."[26] Gladstone, who lived and worked on a horse ranch for two weeks in preparation for the film, adds, "Montanans are infused with landscape. You can sit in a landscape for hours and disappear. You can be part of the quiet. Or you hear the songs of the wind. I remember being hollowed out by the whistle of the wind as a kid. You were at the whim of your landscape and had to live with it."[27] As in Reichardt's other films, the natural environment features prominently in *Certain Women*, and the cast draw effectively upon the landscape to inform their characterization. One quality of Meloy's work that may have attracted Reichardt is the way she paints a picture of Montana, especially the visual roadmap from Glendive to Missoula in the story "Travis, B." As Meloy's central character drives to find Beth, several towns are mentioned by name, and each has characteristics or actions associated with it:

> The road was flat and straight and seemed to roll underneath the truck, dark and silent, through a dark and silent expanse of snow-covered land. He stopped outside of Miles City, and again outside of Billings, to hobble around on his stiffened-up leg until he could drive again. Near Big Timber, the plains ended and the mountains began, black shapes rising up against the stars. He stopped in Bozeman for coffee and gas, and drove the white line on the empty road past Three Forks and Logan, to stay out of the ice that spread from the shoulder in black sheets. Somewhere off to the right in the dark, his parents were sleeping.[28]

Each town comes alive in relation to the character, and readers visit these locations more than once through both Beth's descriptions and the rancher's. Reichardt captures these landscapes even though Jamie only drives to Livingston, halfway on this extended journey. Reichardt ties all three episodes together through location but makes deeper connections via narrative in the last episode as viewers see Laura enter her law firm, dog in tow, while Jamie is requesting Beth's work address from the firm's office associate. Jamie's eyes reflect a pleading and urgent need for direction, and this scene reminds viewers that all four women are not only connected through the landscape, but also by overarching themes of loss and isolation.

Certain Women might be Reichardt's most overt commentary concerning the cultural value placed on women's work. Work is used to form female identities, instead of those identities being based on family or emotional situations, as is more typically seen when introducing women and their stories on screen. Laura's work is questioned and devalued by her male client; only after a male lawyer confirms her opinion does he stop doubting her decisions. Beth Travis, also a lawyer, becomes the office joke because she travels long distances on a dangerous road twice a week to teach in a rural community. Gina, described by her husband as "a boss," is authoritative in almost every scene, but her depiction seems to imply she has sacrificed traditional motherly qualities for her career ambitions. Though all three of these women have advanced education and training in common, none of them appear fulfilled; Reichardt seems to be illustrating the sacrifices and difficulties professional women endure, and how their work is systematically undervalued.

Reichardt also depicts a range of socioeconomic situations and their impact. Beth and Jamie seem to have the most in common: both are from lower-class, socioeconomically challenged families who struggle for opportunity. Beth talks about her mother and sister working in traditionally female stereotyped occupations such as laundry to make ends meet, while she advanced into shoe sales and finally law. Beth not only breaks the glass ceiling of her family's expectations but, like Laura and Gina, occupies a traditionally masculine professional role. Their departure from stereotypically female jobs, not to mention clichéd female emotional responses, is a theme throughout the film; Jamie also occupies a traditionally male job, managing a horse ranch. Jamie's characterization speaks volumes about privilege and class as she watches Beth eat at the local diner twice a week. Clearly she is hungry, since she devours a microwaved mini-hamburger on her drive home; but she never orders, or accepts her instructor's offer of leftover food. Audiences know very little about the rancher except that she "breaks in" horses for fun, and has brothers. Compared to the other women, she represents a lower socioeconomic class. Her youth might play into her life situation, but of all the women it is she, ironically, who seems to take the most emotional chances, despite her extremely repressed state. All the women are emotionally repressed, causing audiences to anticipate an unsettling climax at some point in each episode; but in true Reichardt fashion, those emotions stay simmering just beneath the surface. While all the women physically travel in their episodes, only the rancher appears to take any internal strides. Instead of a return to the status quo, she invites vulnerability and risks rejection by traveling to Livingston in search of Beth. Audiences anticipate action of some consequence, but instead the two women stare at each other in the law office parking lot as the wind whips ruthlessly at them. Reichardt's minimalist and realistic tendencies inform her plot as much as her aesthetic; so as Jamie falls asleep at the wheel during the return trip her gentle departure from the road into a flat field, with no crash, quietly closes the episode.

In *Certain Women*, Reichardt reaches back to her experimental roots with techniques similar to those used in her narrative debut feature, *River of Grass* (1995). Considering *River* was remastered and theatrically rereleased a matter of months before *Certain Women*, it is no surprise that it might have influenced

Reichardt. Both films are segmented or broken up into loose episodes, though the narrative is very different. *River* opens with a prologue and has a continuous narrative with abrupt, random pauses, while *Certain Women* contains an epilogue and three distinct storylines with different characters. Both films are woman-centric and explore either taboo or nontraditional female emotional responses, with male characters and their concerns relegated to the background. *River of Grass* is arguably a dark comedy, and Reichardt revisits this humor in Laura's hostage siege; while the outcome is less violent than in *River*, Laura's client is comical in his attempts to be taken seriously by the police. The tension is defused and Laura's lack of concern makes more sense once audiences realize that he never intended to act on his frustrations. The most striking difference between *Certain Women* and *River*, however, is the stability of the protagonists at the close of the films. Unlike all of Reichardt's previous main characters, Cozy, Kurt, Wendy, Emily and Josh, the characters in *Certain Women* are emotionally and physically stable, with relatively hopeful realities. They are left with multiple possibilities ahead of them rather than the dead ends audiences might predict for many of Reichardt's marginalized protagonists.

During a career that spans over twenty years, Kelly Reichardt has established herself as a contemporary auteur; her micro-budget filmmaking contributes to her techniques and shapes her neorealist and minimalist aesthetic. Through the use of slow cinematic characteristics, she rejects mainstream form and finds an articulate voice for her social and political content. Her pedagogical influence cannot be understated as her work expands the too-narrow scholarly concept of the (male) auteur/indie maverick. The value of exposing students to her production methods and cinematic style could advance the study of women in film. Reichardt offers open if not completely satisfying endings to all her films, and her pacing allows space for reflective and mindful engagement. Through her political and socially conscious film form she reminds viewers, without being didactic, that small, everyday, seemingly mundane acts are what enable individuals to gain insight into the human condition: "Insiders are already well-covered . . . I'm far more interested in the inherent drama of everyday life, the small beats you're constantly up against."[29] Attention to those "small beats" is easily lost in the current age of accelerated cinema, but if Reichardt and other independent contemporary filmmakers continue to celebrate them, audiences are guaranteed to find themselves reflected in their work.

NOTES

1. Reichardt quoted in Iain Blair, "Variety Honoree Kelly Reichardt: Still on the Side of the Outsiders," *Variety Online*, 20 January 2016, <http://variety.com/2016/film/festivals/

variety-honoree-kelly-reichardt-still-on-the-side-of-the-outsiders-1201683518/>
(accessed 20 September 2017).

2. Tatiana Siegel, "Kelly Reichardt's Sundance Title 'Certain Women' Acquired by IFC
   Films," *Hollywood Reporter*, 9 March 2016, <http://www.hollywoodreporter.com/news/
   kelly-reichardts-sundance-title-woman-857403> (accessed 20 September 2017).

3. Gregory Lastra, "Kelly Reichardt's Next Film is an Adaptation of Patrick DeWitt's
   'Undermajordomo Minor,'" *Mxdwn.com*, 1 December 2016, <http://movies.mxdwn.
   com/news/kelly-reichardts-next-film-is-an-adaptation-of-patrick-dewitts-
   undermajordomo-minor/> (accessed 20 September 2017).

4. Neil Kopp, email to author, 15 July 2016; Alice Gregory, "The Quiet Menace of Kelly
   Reichardt's Feminist Westerns," *The New York Times Magazine*, 14 October 2016,
   <http://www.nytimes.com/2016/10/16/magazine/the-quiet-menace-of-kelly-
   reichardts-feminist-westerns.html?_r=0> (accessed 20 September 2017).

5. Kelly Reichardt in discussion with author, 13 July 2015.

6. Paula Bernstein, "Kelly Reichardt on Shooting Certain Women on 16mm," *Filmmaker
   Magazine*, 14 October 2016, <http://filmmakermagazine.com/100081-kelly-reichardt-
   on-shooting-certain-women-on-16mm/> (accessed 20 September 2017).

7. Gregory, "Quiet Menace."

8. Peter Tonguette, "The Wex and the Early Oscar Contender," *Columbus Monthly*, October
   2016, <http://www.columbusmonthly.com/content/stories/2016/10/the-wex-and-the-
   early-oscar-contender.html> (accessed 20 September 2017).

9. Reichardt in discussion with author, 13 July 2015.

10. Linda Hutcheon quoted in Mark Brokenshire, "adaptation," *The Chicago School of Media
    Theory*, <https://lucian.uchicago.edu/blogs/mediatheory/keywords/adaptation/#_
    ftnref10> (accessed 20 September 2017).

11. Jandy, "Adaptation—Rexamining Fidelity Criticism," *The Frame: Cinema Is a Matter of
    What's in the Frame and What's Out* (blog), 18 November 2006, <http://www.the-frame.
    com/2006/11/adaptation-rexamining-fidelity-criticism/> (accessed 14 June 2017).

12. Maile Meloy, "Tome," in *Half in Love: Stories* (New York: Simon and Schuster, 2002),
    Kindle edition.

13. Ibid.

14. Ibid.

15. Maile Meloy, "Native Sandstone," in *Half in Love: Stories*.

16. Maile Meloy, "Travis, B.," in *Both Ways Is the Only Way I Want It* (New York:
    Riverhead Books, 2009), p. 17.

17. Ibid. p. 21.

18. Ibid. p. 3.

19. Ibid. p. 11.

20. Ibid. p. 17.

21. Ibid. p. 23.

22. "Interview with Kelly Reichardt, director of Certain Women," *Culture Whisper*, <https://
    www.culturewhisper.com/r/article/new_kristen_stewart_film_certain_women_director_
    interview/8888> (accessed 20 September 2017).

23. Meloy, "Travis, B.," p. 3.

24. Ibid. p. 6.

25. Kate Kellaway, "Lily Gladstone: 'I lived in the reservations until I was 11,'" *The
    Guardian*, 12 February 2017, <https://www.theguardian.com/film/2017/feb/12/lily-
    gladstone-interview-certain-women-kristen-stewart-kelly-reichardt> (accessed 20
    September 2017).

26. Reichardt quoted in ibid.
27. Ibid.
28. Meloy, "Travis, B.," p. 19.
29. Reichardt quoted in Blair, "Variety Honoree Kelly Reichardt."

An Interview with Kelly Reichardt

In the summer of 2015, Kelly Reichardt agreed to discuss career and production details with me in an effort to inform this book and provide insight into her latest film.

Phone interview on the campus of Western Kentucky University, June 2015
Interviewers: E. Dawn Hall and Allison Adams

DH: In *River of Grass*, was the character of Ryder loosely based on your father?

KR: No, Ryder is not anything like my dad; the connections were very superficial. The film was shot in a neighborhood where I've lived for some years, and my dad was a crime scene detective, but that's about the extent of the autobiography bits of it.

DH: Do any other people that you know pop up as characters in your films or in your writing?

KR: No. Part of what's great about making a film is stepping into a world that isn't your own. It's great to get away from yourself and learn about some scene that isn't quite your own. It doesn't mean it isn't relatable, but it's outside of what's familiar.

DH: In all of your films, is there a purposeful emphasis on environmentalism that culminated in *Night Moves*, or did that emphasis just evolve? Were issues surrounding the environment in your consciousness?

KR: With *Night Moves*, Jon Raymond wanted to write a script about a group of fundamentalists and instead of looking to the right, he wrote about these young lefty radicals—people with a more relatable and, to our eyes, a more justified agenda. Environmentalism is at the core of the character's concerns and the motivating factor (at least on some level) for blowing up this dam. So issues of the environment are front and center because these characters are living on an organic farm and attending meetings about political activism—these are the issues they are focused on.

DH: Speaking of *Night Moves*, when I was at the theater there was an audible reaction to the ending. When it goes black the entire theater just either sighs, or they gasp. Did you write it that way, or did it just happen that way in the editing room?

KR: That's how it was scripted.

DH: In the chapter on *Night Moves*, I suggest that the ending of *Night Moves* is the most hopeless of all the films. Mainly, because Josh is staring at that job application and he's going into a world that he's been trying to leave.

KR: Right. Well, my dear colleague Peter Hutton, who we lost this month, and who is someone I'm really going to miss talking about films with—who I miss terribly in general. I just found an old email he had written me about the films all being about futility. In *Meek's* it's left to the audience to decide if there is a good ending to come or a bad ending, and *River of Grass* is more open too. *Night Moves* isn't as open for interpretation.

DH: It seems in all of your films, including the shorts, there is an underlying political commentary. Is it a conscious decision to insert politics while you are writing or adapting scripts, or is it just organic to the story?

KR: Generally speaking, things don't just happen. Conceiving a story, writing a script and making a film—these are all long-drawn-out processes. I think what drew me to the Jon Raymond stories is his ability to write politically without writing politically. There's no message in a Raymond story, no clear ideological path. It's all murky territory, and murky is more of a challenge than a straight shot to something. Ultimately they are all character films.

AA: If possible I'd like to focus on script and adaptation writing for a moment. You have so many silences in your films and you work with so much internal character development, so what do your scripts look like? How do you incorporate silences?

KR: We're often pulling dialogue out as we go. It's a visual medium so a lot of the process is figuring out how it can happen through camera placement or through a cut, a gesture or pause. Sometimes an actor does something in a rehearsal right before we shoot that reveals a moment in a different way . We work from a script and I come with a plan because we move very quickly and our budgets don't allow us a lot of time. But the film has a life of its own and opportunities reveal themselves as you go.

DH: As you've said before, filming on a limited budget is hard. You have to be creative and inventive. Does it wear you down?

KR: We have pushed ourselves to, possibly, the brink. The remote landscapes are very difficult. Shooting outside in the winter is difficult.

DH: I know we have to wrap up, so one last question. What filmmakers do you make an effort to follow? Is there anything that has caught your eye, or trends you are moving towards?

KR: I've been revisiting Peter Hutton's films because I miss him. He made films without a lot of movement and without any sound—he called himself the "rear guard." His films keep reminding us about how to really look and use your eyes—the difference in letting a viewer see something as opposed to showing it to them.

Filmography

Bicycle Thieves, dir. Vittorio De Sica, feat. Lamberto Maggiorani, Enzo Staiola, Lianella Carell (Produzioni De Sica, 1948).
Bonnie and Clyde, dir. Arthur Penn, feat. Warren Beatty, Faye Dunaway, Michael J. Pollard (Warner Brothers/Seven Arts, 1967).
The Bourne Ultimatum, dir. Paul Greengrass, feat. Matt Damon, Edgar Ramírez, Joan Allen (Universal Pictures, 2007).
Certain Women, dir. Kelly Reichardt, feat. Michelle Williams, Kristen Stewart, Laura Dern (Filmscience, 2016).
Clerks, dir. Kevin Smith, feat. Brian O'Halloran, Jeff Anderson, Marilyn Ghigliotti (View Askew Productions, 1994).
The 400 Blows, dir. François Truffaut, feat. Jean-Pierre Léaud, Albert Rémy, Claire Maurier (Les Films du Carrosse, 1959).
Frozen River, dir. Courtney Hunt, feat. Melissa Leo, Misty Upham (Cohen Media Group, 2008).
If a Tree Falls, dir. Marshall Curry and Sam Cullman, feat. Daniel McGowan, Lisa McGowan, Tim Lewis (Marshall Curry Productions LLC, 2011).
Meek's Cutoff, dir. Kelly Reichardt, feat. Michelle Williams, Bruce Greenwood, Paul Dano (Evenstar Films, 2010).
Natural Born Killers, dir. Oliver Stone, feat. Woody Harrelson, Juliette Lewis, Tom Sizemore (Warner Brothers, 1994).
Night Moves, dir. Kelly Reichardt, feat. Jesse Eisenberg, Dakota Fanning, Peter Sarsgaard (Maybach Films, 2013).
North by Northwest, dir. Alfred Hitchcock, feat. Cary Grant, Eva Marie Saint, James Mason (Metro-Goldwyn-Mayer, 1959).
Ode, dir. Kelly Reichardt, feat. Kevin Poole, Bill Mooney, Heather Gottlieb (1999).
Old Joy, dir. Kelly Reichardt, feat. Daniel London, Will Oldham, Tanya Smith (Filmscience, 2006).
Poison, dir. Todd Haynes, feat. Edith Meeks, Larry Maxwell, Susan Norman (Bronze Eye Productions, 1991).
Psycho, dir. Alfred Hitchcock, feat. Anthony Perkins, Janet Leigh, Vera Mills (Shamley Productions, 1960).

River of Grass, dir. Kelly Reichardt, feat. Lisa Bowman, Larry Fessenden, Dick Russell (Good Machine, 1994).

Spanking the Monkey, dir. David O. Russell, feat. Jeremy Davies, Alberta Watson, Elizabeth Newett (Buckeye Films, 1994).

Strike, dir. Sergei Eisenstein, feat. Grigoriy Aleksandrov, Maksim Shtraukh, Mikhail Gomorov (Goskino, 1925).

Then, a Year, dir. Kelly Reichardt (2001).

Travis, dir. Kelly Reichardt (2004).

Umberto D., dir. Vittorio De Sica, feat. Carlo Battisti, Maria Pia Casilio, Lina Gennari (Rizzoli Film, 1952).

The Unbelievable Truth, dir. Hal Hartley, feat. Adrienne Shelly, Robert John Burke, Chris Cooke (Action Features, 1989).

Wendy and Lucy, dir. Kelly Reichardt, feat. Michelle Williams, Lucy, David Koppell (Field Guide Films, 2008).

Winter's Bone, dir. Debra Granik, feat. Jennifer Lawrence, John Hawkes (Anonymous Content, 2010).

Zero Dark Thirty, dir. Kathryn Bigelow, feat. Jessica Chastain, Joel Edgerton, Chris Pratt (Columbia Pictures, 2011).

Bibliography

"About Us," Cinetic Media, <https://www.cineticmedia.com/about-us> (accessed 20 September 2017).

Adams, Mark (2010), "Meek's Cutoff," *Screendaily*, 6 September, <http://www.screendaily.com/reviews /latest-reviews/-meeks-cutoff/5017812.article#> (accessed 20 September 2017).

Adams, Sam (2011), "Kelly Reichardt and Jon Raymond," The A.V. Club, 26 April, <https://film.avclub.com/kelly-reichardt-and-jon-raymond-1798225326> (accessed 20 September 2017).

Aguilar, Rose (2013), interviewed by Robin Young, *Here and Now*, National Public Radio WBUR, 25 February.

Altman, Rick (1999), *Film/Genre* (London: BFI).

Arizzi, Erin Marie (2015), "Modeling Professional Femininity Through U.S. Media Culture, 1963–2015," Ph.D. dissertation, <http://search.proquest.com/docview/1755656600/> (accessed 20 September 2017).

Associated Press (2008), "Company Creates Hard-to-Ignite Fertilizer to Foil Bomb-Makers," *Fox News*, 23 September, <http://www.foxnews.com/story/2008/09/23/company-creates-hard-to-ignite-fertilizer-to-foil-bomb-makers.html?sPage=fnc/scitech/naturalscience> (accessed 20 September 2017).

Bazin, André (1999), "The Myth of Total Cinema," in Leo Braudy and Marshall Cohen (eds.), *Film Theory and Criticism*, 5th edn., New York: Oxford University Press, pp. 199–203.

Bernstein, Paula (2016), "Kelly Reichardt on Shooting Certain Women on 16mm, the Ugliness of the Day, and Making the Space Tell the Story," *Filmmaker Magazine*, 14 October, <http://filmmakermagazine.com/100081-kelly-reichardt-on-shooting-certain-women-on-16mm/#.WFmmLVMrJoy> (accessed 20 September 2017).

Blair, Iain (2016), "Variety Honoree Kelly Reichardt: Still on the Side of the Outsiders," *Variety Online*, 20 January, <http://variety.com/2016/film/festivals/variety-honoree-kelly-reichardt-still-on-the-side-of-the-outsiders-1201683518/> (accessed 20 September 2017).

Butler, Judith (2003), "Performative Acts and Gender Constitution: An Essay in

Phenomenology and Feminist Theory," in Amelia Jones (ed.), *The Feminism and Visual Culture Reader*, London: Routledge.

Cerridwen, Anemone and Dean K. Simonton (2009), "Sex Doesn't Sell—Nor Impress! Content, Box Office, Critics, and Awards in Mainstream Cinema," *Psychology of Aesthetics, Creativity and the Arts* 3, no. 4 (2009): 200–10, <https://www.apa.org/pubs/journals/releases/aca-3-4-200.pdf> (accessed 17 September 2017).

"*Certain Women*," *Box Office Mojo*, <http://www.boxofficemojo.com/movies/?page=weekly &id=certainwomen.htm> (accessed 20 September 2017).

Chaudhuri, Shohini, and Howard Finn (2006), "The Open Image: Poetic Realism and the New Iranian Cinema," in Annette Kuhn and Catherine Grant (eds.), *Screening World Cinema*, New York and London: Routledge.

"*Cold Case Files—Vanished*" (2010), ArkTV.com.

Cook, Pam, ed. (2007), *The Cinema Book*, 3rd edn., London: British Film Institute.

Dargis, Manohla (2006), "A Journey Through Forests and a Sense of Regret," *The New York Times*, 20 September, <http://www.nytimes.com/2006/09/20/movies/a-journey-through-forests-and-a-sense-of-regret.html> (accessed 20 September 2017).

Dargis, Manohla, and A. O. Scott (2011), "In Defense of the Slow and the Boring," *The New York Times*, 3 June, <http://www.nytimes.com/2011/06/05/movies/films-in-defense-of-slow-and-boring.html> (accessed 20 September 2017).

Dunn, Jamie (2011), "Kelly Reichardt: Redefining the Western," *The Skinny*, 7 April, <http://www.theskinny.co.uk/film/interviews/kelly-reichardt-redefining-the-western> (accessed 20 September 2017).

Earth Liberation Front, <http://earth-liberation-front.com/> (accessed 17 April 2017).

Esther, John (2006), "GLBT Films Keep Comin' At Sundance '06," *The Gay & Lesbian Review Worldwide* 13, no. 3.

Ficks, Jesse Hawthorne (2011), "Northwest Passage: Kelly Reichardt on 'Meek's Cutoff,'" *San Francisco Bay Guardian Online*, 3 May, <http://48hills.org/sfbgarchive/2011/05/03/northwest-passage-kelly-reichardt-meeks-cutoff/> (accessed 20 September 2017).

Flanagan, Matthew (2008), "Towards an Aesthetic of Slow in Contemporary Cinema," *16:9 Film Journal* 6, no. 29, <http://www.16-9.dk/2008-11/side11_inenglish.htm> (accessed 20 September 2017).

Friedan, Betty (1963), *The Feminine Mystique*, New York: Norton.

Fuller, Graham (2011), "The Oregon Trail," *Sight And Sound* 21, no. 5: 38–42.

Gaard, Greta (2010), "New Directions for Ecofeminism: Toward a More Feminist Ecocriticism," *Interdisciplinary Studies in Literature and Environment* 17, no. 4: 643–65.

Gilbey, Ryan (2011), "Kelly Reichardt: How I Trekked Across Oregon for *Meek's Cutoff* Then Returned to Teaching," *The Guardian*, 8 April, <https://www.theguardian.com/film/2011/apr/09/kelly-reichardt-meeks-cutoff> (accessed 20 September 2017).

Gills, Melina (2014), "Kelly Reichardt On Directing 'Night Moves,' Editing Her Own Films, and Shooting in Living Spaces," *IndieWire*, 30 May, <http://www.indiewire.com/2014/05/kelly-reichardt-on-directing-night-moves-editing-her-own-films-and-shooting-in-living-spaces-25945/> (accessed 20 September 2017).

Gledhill, Christine (1994), "Image and Voice: Approaches to Marxist-Feminist Film Criticism," in Diane Carson et al. (eds.), *Multiple Voices*, Minneapolis: University of Minnesota Press.

Gray, Jerry (1995), "Senate Votes to Aid Tracing of Explosives," *The New York Times*, 6 June, <http://www.nytimes.com/1995/06/06/us/senate-votes-to-aid-tracing-ofexplosives.html> (accessed 20 September 2017).

Green, David (2002), "Dude, Where's My Gender? Contemporary Teen Comedies and New Forms of American Masculinity," *Cineaste* 27, no. 3: 14–21.

Gregory, Alice (2016), "The Quiet Menace of Kelly Reichardt's Feminist Westerns," *The New York Times Magazine*, 14 October, <http://www.nytimes.com/2016/10/16/magazine/the-quiet-menace-of-kelly-reichardts-feminist-westerns.html?_r=0> (accessed 20 September 2017).

Harris, Anita (2004), *Future Girl: Young Women in the Twenty-First Century*, New York: Routledge.

Haynes, Todd (1995), "Kelly Reichardt," *Bomb* 53, <http://bombmagazine.org/article/1891/kelly-reichardt> (accessed 20 September 2017).

Hernandez, Eugene (2014), "Kelly Reichardt Q&A: *Night Moves*" (Film Society of Lincoln Center interview, 31 July), <https://www.youtube.com/watch?v=18zzyN9FRew> (accessed 20 September 2017).

Hollinger, Karen (2012), *Feminist Film Studies*, New York: Routledge.

Holt, Jeff (2009), "A Summary of the Primary Causes of the Housing Bubble and the Resulting Credit Crisis: A Non-Technical Paper," *The Journal of Business Inquiry* (2009): 120–9.

Hornaday, Ann (2011), "Director Kelly Reichardt on 'Meek's Cutoff' and making movies her way," *Washington Post*, 12 May, <https://www.washingtonpost.com/lifestyle/style/director-kelly-reichardt-on-meeks-cutoff-and-making-movies-her-way/2011/05/08/AFOl0K7G_story.html> (accessed 20 September 2017).

"Interview with Kelly Reichardt, director of Certain Women," *Culture Whisper*, <https://www.culturewhisper.com/r/ruiicle/new_kristen_stewart_film_certain_women_director_interview/8888> (accessed 20 September 2017).

"James R. Hicks," *Murderpedia.org*, <http://murderpedia.org/male.H/h/hicks-james.htm> (accessed 20 September 2017).

Jenkins, David, and Nick James (2014), "The Dam Busters," *Sight & Sound* 24, no. 9: 56–9.

Joseph, Jennifer et al. (2015), "Mary Kay Letourneau Fualaau, Vili Fualaau Detail Their Path from Teacher-Student Sex Scandal to Raising Teenagers," *ABCNews.com.*, <http://abcnews.go.com/US/mary-kay-letourneau-fualaau-vili-fualaau-detail-path/story?id=30160737> (accessed 20 September 2017).

Kaplan, Ann E. (1988), *Women and Film: Both Sides of the Camera*, New York: Methuen.

Kauffmann, Stanley (2006), "Parting Of Ways," *New Republic* 235, no. 14: 28–9.

Kellaway, Kate (2017), "Lily Gladstone: 'I lived in the reservations until I was 11,'" *The Guardian*, 12 February, <https://www.theguardian.com/film/2017/feb/12/lilygladstone-interview-certain-women-kristen-stewart-kelly-reichardt> (accessed 20 September 2017).

"Kelly Reichardt" (2012), *This Long Century*, no. 190, <http://www.thislongcentury.com/?p=5570> (accessed 20 September 2017).

Kimmel, Michael (2004), "Masculinity as Homophobia," in Estelle Disch (ed.), *Reconstructing Gender: A Multicultural Anthology*, 3rd edn., Boston: McGraw Hill.

Kimmel, Michael (2005), *The History of Men*, New York: State University of New York Press.

Lastra, Gregory (2016), "Kelly Reichardt's Next Film is an Adaptation of Patrick DeWitt's 'Undermajordomo Minor.'" *Mxdwn.com*, 1 December, <http://movies.mxdwn.com/news/kelly-reichardts-next-film-is-an-adaptation-of-patrick-dewitts-undermajordomo-minor/> (accessed 20 September 2017).

Lattimer, James (2011), "Beyond Neo-Neo Realism: Reconfigurations of Neorealist Narration in Kelly Reichardt's *Meek's Cutoff*," *Cinephile* 7, no. 2: 37–41.

Liu, David (2010), "It Takes a Train to Cry: The Cinema of Kelly Reichardt," *Kino Obscura*,

19 November, <http://kino-obscura.com/post/1619587333/it-takes-a- train-to-cry> (accessed 20 September 2017).

Liu, David (2012), "In Conversation: Kelly Reichardt," *Kino Obscura*, 20 August, <http:// kino-obscura.com/post/30205580824/in-conversation-kelly-reichardt> (accessed 20 September 2017).

Longworth, Karina (2011), "Kelly Reichardt Explains 'Meek's Cutoff,' Her Latest Road Movie," *San Francisco Weekly*, 4 May, <https://archives.sfweekly.com/sanfrancisco/kelly-reichardt-explains-meeks-cutoff-her-latest-road-movie/Content?oid=2181363> (accessed 20 September 2017).

Marks, Laura (2000), *The Skin of the Film: Intercultural Cinema, Embodiment, and The Senses*, Durham, NC: Duke University Press.

McCrisken, Trevor B. (2002), "Exceptionalism: Manifest Destiny," in *Encyclopedia of American Foreign Policy*, New York: Scribner.

"Meek's Cutoff," Box Office Mojo, <http://www.boxofficemojo.com/movies/?id=meekscutoff. htm> (accessed 20 September 2017).

Meek's Cutoff (2010): "Awards," *Internet Movie Database*, <http://www.imdb.com/title/ tt1518812/awards?ref_=tt_ql_op_1> (accessed 20 September 2017).

Meloy, Maile (2002a), "Native Sandstone." *Half in Love: Stories*, New York: Simon and Schuster.

Meloy, Maile (2002b), "Tome." *Half in Love: Stories*, New York: Simon and Schuster.

Meloy, Maile (2009), "Travis, B." *Both Ways Is the Only Way I Want It*, New York: Riverhead Books.

Murphy, J. J. (2009), *"River of Grass,"* blog post, 22 July, <http://www.jjmurphyfilm.com/ blog/2009/07/22/river-of-grass/> (accessed 20 September 2017).

Mulvey, Laura (1975), "Visual Pleasure and Narrative Cinema," *Screen* 16, no. 3: 6–18.

Newman, Michael (2011), *Indie: An American Film Culture*, ed. John Benton, New York: Columbia University Press.

"Night Moves," Box Office Mojo,< http://www.boxofficemojo.com/movies/?id=nightmoves. htm> (accessed 20 September 2017).

Night Moves: "Awards," *Internet Movie Database*, <http://www.imdb.com/title/tt2043933/ awards?ref_=tt_ql_op_1> (accessed 20 September 2017).

"Occupy Wall Street: A Protest Timeline" (2016), *The Week*, 21 July, <http://theweek.com/ articles/481160/occupy-wall-street-protest-timeline> (accessed 20 September 2017).

Office of the Press Secretary (2011), "Secretary Napolitano Announces Proposed Ammonium Nitrate Security Program," Department of Homeland Security, <https://www.dhs.gov/ news/2011/08/02/secretary-napolitano-announces-proposed-ammonium-nitrate-security-program> (accessed 20 September 2017).

"Old Joy" (2006): Awards," *Internet Movie Database*, <http://www.imdb.com/title/ tt0468526/awards?ref_=tt_awd> (accessed 20 September 2017).

"Old Joy—Daniel London and Kelly Reichardt Interview" (2007), YouTube video posted by DDC Collective, 8 August, <https://www.youtube.com/watch?v=RKJgxh3PQDM> (accessed 20 September 2017).

Oppermann, Serpil (2013), "Feminist Ecocriticism: The New Ecofeminist Settlement," *Feminismo/s: Special Issue on Ecofeminism*: 1–19.

Ortner, Sherry (2013), *Not Hollywood: Independent Film at the Twilight of the American Dream*, Durham, NC: Duke University Press.

Patten, Dominic (2012), "'Night Moves' Director, Producers, UTA Sued By Edward Pressman & Edward Abbey Widow For Copyright Infringement," *Deadline Hollywood*, 15 September, <http://deadline.com/2012/09/

uta-director-kelly-reichardt-sued-byedwardpressman-edward-abbey-widow-for-copyright-infringement-336968/> (accessed 20 September 2017).

Plante, Mike (2011), "Kelly Reichardt: Meet the Artist," *Sundance Film Festival*.

Ponsoldt, James (2011), "Lost in America: Kelly Reichardt's 'Meek's Cutoff,'" *Filmmaker Magazine*, November 2011, <http://filmmakermagazine.com/35034-lost-in-america-kelly-reichardts-meeks-cutoff/#.WGQDIlMrJow> (accessed 20 September 2017).

Raymond, Jon (2009), "Train Choir," in *Livability*, New York: Bloomsbury.

Reichardt, Kelly (2011), "*Old Joy* Director's Statement," Museum of the Moving Image Series *Adrift in America: The Films of Kelly Reichardt*, 3 April.

Reichardt, Kelly, and Michelle Williams (2008), "Wendy and Lucy Q&A: Kelly Reichardt and Michelle Williams," *Filmlinc.com*, 4 October.

"*River of Grass* (1994): Awards," *Internet Movie Database*, <http://www.imdb.com/title/tto110998/awards?ref_=tt_ql_op_1> (accessed 20 September 2017).

Rodriguez-Ortega, Vicente (2006), "New Voice: An Interview with Kelly Reichardt," *Reverse Shot*, 18 September, <http://reverseshot.org/interviews/entry/804/kelly-reichardt> (accessed 20 September 2017).

Romney, Jonathan (2010), "In Search of Lost Time," *Sight and Sound* 20, no. 2: 43–4.

Rose, Jennie (2011), "Women in Film," *GreenCine*, 3 December.

Rowin, Michael Joshua (2006), "Q & A: Kelly Reichardt, Director of *Old Joy*," *Stop Smiling Magazine*, 22 September, <http://www.stopsmilingonline.com/story_detail.php?id=655> (accessed 20 September 2017).

Rugh, Peter (2016), "Building a Radical Environmental Movement," *Occupy Wall Street*, <http://occupywallstreet.net/story/building-radical-environmental-movement> (accessed 20 September 2017).

Saito, Stephen (2011), "Kelly Reichardt on Surviving 'Meek's Cutoff,'" *IFC*, 22 April, <http://www.ifc.com/2011/04/kelly-reichardt-meeks-cutoff> (accessed 20 September 2017).

Sandhu, Sukhdev (2012), "'Slow cinema' fights back against Bourne's supremacy," *The Guardian*, 9 March, <https://www.theguardian.com/film/2012/mar/09/slow-cinema-fights-bournes-supremacy> (accessed 20 September 2017).

Savjani, Anish, interviewed by Eren Gulfidan (2008), "Interview with Anish Savjani, the producer of *Wendy and Lucy*," *Film Annex*, 19 January.

Scott, A. O. (2009), "Neo-Neo Realism," *The New York Times Magazine*, 17 March, <http://www.nytimes.com/2009/03/22/magazine/22neorealism-t.html?pagewanted=all> (accessed 20 September 2017).

Shapiro, Ari (2012), *Talk of The Nation*, National Public Radio, 6 December.

Sholis, Brian (2008), "Interview with Kelly Reichardt," *Artforum*, October, <https://www.artforum.com/inprint/issue=200808&id=21124> (accessed 20 September 2017).

Sicinski, Michael (2009), "*Wendy and Lucy*," *Cineaste*, <https://www.cineaste.com/spring2009/wendy-and-lucy/> (accessed 20 September 2017).

Siegel, Tatiana (2016), "Kelly Reichardt's Sundance Title 'Certain Women' Acquired by IFC Films," *Hollywood Reporter*, 9 March, <http://www.hollywoodreporter.com/news/kelly-reichardts-sundance-title-woman-857403> (accessed 20 September 2017).

Silberg, Jon (2014), "Spotlight: Christopher Blauvelt," *Digital Video* 22, no. 6: 16, <http://www.creativeplanetnetwork.com/news/orphaned-articles/spotlight-christopher-blauvelt-cinematographer-night-moves/605620> (accessed 20 September 2017).

Stewart, Ryan (2008), "Redefining Success: An Interview with Kelly Reichardt." *Slant Magazine*, 5 December, <https://www.slantmagazine.com/features/article/redefining-success-an-interview-with-kelly-reichardt> (accessed 20 September 2017).

Taylor, Ella (2011), "'Meek's Cutoff': An Old West, Captured for a New Era." National Public Radio, 7 April.

Thompson, Anne (2011), "Meek's Cutoff: Professor Kelly Reichardt's Filmmaking 101 Primer," *IndieWire*, 21 April.

Thompson, Steve, and Reese Dunklin (2013), "Ammonium Nitrate Sold by Ton as U.S. Regulation Is Stymied," *The Dallas Morning News*, October, <https://www.dallasnews.com/news/news/2013/10/05/ammonium-nitrate-sold-by-ton-as-u.s.-regulation-is-stymied> (accessed 20 September 2017).

Tonguette, Peter (2016), "The Wex and the Early Oscar Contender," *Columbus Monthly*, October, <http://www.columbusmonthly.com/content/stories/2016/10/the-wex-and-the-early-oscar-contender.html> (accessed 20 September 2017).

Toumarkine, Doris (2009), "Lab Results: Oscilloscope Tests Today's Market With Cost-Effective Strategies," *Film Journal International* 112, no.10: 8–26.

Tuana, Nancy (2008), "Viscous Porosity: Witnessing Katrina," in Stacy Alaimo and Susan Hekman (eds.), *Material Feminism*, Bloomington: Indiana University Press (2008), pp. 188–213.

Vadim, Rizov (2010), "Slow Cinema Backlash," <http://www.ifc.com/2010/05/slow-cinemabacklash> (accessed 20 September 2017).

"Victims of the Oklahoma City Bombing" (2001), *USA Today*, 20 June, <https://usatoday30.usatoday.com/news/nation/2001-06-11-mcveigh-victims.htm> (accessed 20 September 2017).

Van Sant, Gus (2008), "Artists in Conversation: Kelly Reichardt," *Bomb* 105: 76–81, <http://bombmagazine.org/article/3182/kelly-reichardt> (accessed 20 September 2017).

"*Wendy and Lucy*," *Box Office Mojo*, <http://www.boxofficemojo.com/movies/?id=wendyandlucy.htm> (accessed 20 September 2017).

"*Wendy and Lucy* (2008): Awards," *Internet Movie Database*, <http://www.imdb.com/title/tt1152850/awards?ref_=tt_awd> (accessed 20 September 2017).

Wertz, Joe (2014), "Mapped: Oklahoma's Dams and the Potential Hazards They Pose," *State Impact*, 12 December <https://stateimpact.npr.org/oklahoma/2014/12/12/mapped-oklahomas-dams-and-the-potential-hazards-they-pose/> (accessed 20 September 2017).

Wilhite, Donald A. (n. d.), "Dust Bowl," in *The Encyclopedia of Oklahoma History and Culture*, <http://www.okhistory.org/publications/enc/entry.php?entry=du011> (accessed 20 September 2017).

Williams, Michelle, interviewed by S. T. Vanairsdale (2011), "Michelle Williams on *Meek's Cutoff*, Goodbyes and Getting Lost at the Movies," *MovieLine*, 30 March, <http://movieline.com/2011/03/30/michelle-williams-on-meeks-cutoff-goodbyes-and-getting-lost-at-the-movies/> (accessed 20 September 2017).

Williams, Michelle, and Kelly Reichardt, interviewed by Terry Gross (2011), "Going West: the Making of 'Meek's Cutoff,'" *Fresh Air*, National Public Radio WHYY, 4 April.

Wollen, Peter (1999), "Godard and Counter Cinema: *Vent d'Est*," in Leo Braudy and Marshall Cohen (eds.), *Film Theory and Criticism*, 5th edn., New York: Oxford University Press, pp. 499–508.

Woodward, Adam (2011), "Kelly Reichardt Review," *Little White Lies*.

Index

CPSIA information can be obtained
at www.ICGtesting.com
Printed in the USA
JSHW031048250321
12899JS00004B/266